Look Who's Talking!

A Comedy

Derek Benfield

A SAMUEL FRENCH ACTING EDITION

SAMUEL
FRENCH
FOUNDED 1830

SAMUELFRENCH-LONDON.CO.UK
SAMUELFRENCH.COM

FOR AMATEUR PRODUCTION ENQUIRIES

UNITED KINGDOM AND WORLD
EXCLUDING NORTH AMERICA
plays@SamuelFrench-London.co.uk
020 7255 4302/01

Each title is subject to availability from Samuel French,

depending upon country of performance.

LOOK WHO'S TALKING!

First presented by Mark Furness on a national tour which opened at the Wyvern Theatre, Swindon, on April 26th 1983, with the following cast of characters:

Sheila	Hilary Tindall
Brian	Christopher Strauli
Andrew	Donald Hewlett
Carole	Ava Healy
Jane	Miranda Forbes

The play directed by Charles Savage
Setting by Donald Crosby

The play takes place in the drawing-room of Sheila's and Andrew's comfortable home in the country

ACT I   A Sunday morning in the summer
ACT II   The same. A few minutes later

Time—the present

Other plays by Derek Benfield
published by Samuel French Ltd

Bedside Manners
Beyond a Joke
A Bird In The Hand
Caught On The Hop
Fish Out Of Water
Flying Feathers
In For The Kill
Murder For the Asking
Off The Hook!
Panic Stations
Post Horn Gallop
Running Riot
Touch and Go
Wild Goose Chase

ACT I

The drawing-room of Andrew's and Sheila's detached house in the country. A Sunday morning in the summer: the sun is shining

Two steps lead up to large sliding glass doors, through which there is a delightful view of the garden, and a paved patio with garden furniture and an abundance of potted plants. A brightly-coloured sun umbrella stands unopened nearby. Swing doors lead out to the kitchen, where we get an occasional glimpse of various kitchen units. An archway leads out to the hall and the front door. An oval dining-table stands against the wall below the archway with four dining chairs set around it. There is a large, comfortable sofa and various other tables, etc. The setting is pleasant and tasteful, and the furniture expensive

The Sunday papers lie haphazardly on the sofa, and a portable transistor radio on the sofa table is emitting relaxing light music. (Ideally, a vocal version of "Sunday, Sweet Sunday" from "Flower Drum Song")

Sheila comes in from the kitchen, wearing a striped apron over her dress. She has a glass-cloth over her arm and carries three wine glasses. Sheila is an attractive woman, with her upper-class life ordered and comfortable. She goes to the table to set out the glasses

Brian appears out on the patio, looking about, obviously seeing it all for the first time. He is a cheerful, good-looking man, a few years younger than Sheila. He is carrying a bunch of flowers

Sheila does not see him. But he sees her all right! He smiles, tiptoes into the room, watching as she polishes the glasses and sets them out

She goes out to the kitchen, without noticing him, and returns with some cutlery. She goes to the table again

Brian tiptoes to the radio and switches it off. Sheila turns in surprise and sees him.

Sheila Brian! (*Then she drops some of the cutlery*)

He just looks at her and smiles

Brian Hallo . . .
Sheila Oh, good heavens . . .! (*She bends down to pick up the cutlery, hastily trying to conceal her obvious recognition of him*)
Brian Well—here I am! (*He holds out the bunch of flowers with a flourish*)

Sheila stands up and stares at the flowers for a moment in silence. Then . . .

Sheila Are you looking for my husband?

Brian (*glancing at the flowers, amused*) Well, I don't usually give flowers to men. They're for *you*.

Sheila (*abruptly*) What?

Brian Aren't you going to take them?

Sheila I'm not in the habit of accepting flowers from any strange Tom, Dick or Harry who wanders into my house.

Brian (*grinning, amiably*) I'm not a stranger! And *you* know my name isn't Tom, Dick or Harry.

Sheila D-do I?

Brian Well, you called me Brian just now.

Sheila (*floundering*) I—I can't think why I did that.

Brian moves closer to her with a penetrating smile.

Brian Why are you pretending you don't know me?

Sheila I'm not pretending! Look—if you've come to read the gas meter it's under the stairs.

Brian Read the gas meter on a Sunday? (*He laughs*) Oh, no—I'm not here for that.

Sheila Aren't you?

Brian Certainly not! (*He holds out the flowers again*) Well, go on—take them.

Sheila tries to escape under the mantle of assumed outrage.

Sheila Look—this is private property! You have no right to come barging in here with a bunch of flowers. (*She hastens back to the table and starts to polish the cutlery briskly with the glass-cloth, deliberately avoiding his eyes*)

Brian watches her with a smile, and moves, purposefully, across to just behind her.

Brian Sheila—!

Sheila (*jumping nervously*) Aah! Don't creep up on me like that!

Brian You're not nervous, are you?

Sheila Why should I be nervous? Go away, or I'll call the police! (*She sets off for the kitchen again*)

Brian Aren't you going to put these in water?

Sheila Certainly not! They're nothing to do with *me*!

She goes out into the kitchen, then reappears immediately.

If any of the silver disappears I'll have you arrested.

She disappears back into the kitchen.

Brian shrugs and puts the bunch of flowers down on the sofa table.

Brian (*calling*) Do you mind if I sit down? It's a bit of a trek up from the station. (*Getting no reply, he sits on the sofa anyway and looks at a magazine*)

Sheila comes back with the pepper and salt. She sees him on the sofa and reacts in alarm.

Sheila You're sitting on my sofa!

Brian What?

Sheila You've no right to be sitting on my sofa! (*She goes to the table, puts down the pepper and salt, and starts to lay the cutlery, evasively*)

Brian (*gazing at her, adoringly*) You know . . . you're even more attractive than I remember.

Sheila drops a fork, nervously, casts an anxious glance towards the garden and goes to him, urgently.

Sheila Look—I think you've been here quite long enough. Will you please go! (*She tries to pull him to his feet*)

Brian looks at her in surprise

Brian But I've only just arrived.

Sheila Well, you can't stay here!

Brian Why not?

Sheila Because there's someone coming to lunch.

Brian Yes. *Me!*

Sheila No. Someone else.

Brian Oh, dear. I did rather hope we were dining alone. (*He grins*) Oh, come on—you're just teasing! Of course we're dining alone. I tell you what—I'll go and peel the potatoes. (*He gets up and goes towards the kitchen*) Through here, is it?

Sheila The potatoes are already done.

Brian Really?

Sheila Mrs Garbut did them last night.

Brian Good old Mrs Garbut! I'll just do some more for me then. (*He starts to go*)

Sheila You won't be staying for lunch!

Brian But I've come all the way from Amersham.

Sheila Then I suggest you go back there at once. Come on! (*She urges him on his way*) Off you go!

Brian Why are you pretending you don't remember?

Sheila (*evasively*) I don't know what you mean. There's nothing *to* remember.

Brian Nothing to remember? (*With heavy innuendo*) About Friday evening?

Sheila *I* don't remember anything about Friday evening.

Brian I'm not surprised! The wine was good, wasn't it? (*He smiles, remembering*)

Sheila What do *you* know about the wine? (*She shifts, uneasily, under his penetrating gaze*) I . . . I don't like the way you smile. It's . . . it's suggestive. (*She escapes from the smile and goes to get the table napkins*)

Brian I'm sorry. I'll try not to do it again. It's not surprising, though, is it? After what we did together on Friday evening . . .

Sheila We didn't do anything! (*She starts to fold the napkins in a desultory manner*)

Brian We drank some wine.

Sheila Did we?

Brian *And* we got talking. You know how it is . . .

Sheila No, I do *not* know how it is!

Brian I said this, and you said that, and . . . and that's how it happened.

Sheila Nothing happened!

Brian (*triumphantly*) Ah-ha! You said you didn't remember!

Sheila I'd remember *that*! Look—I was having dinner on Friday, and I know who I was with and it wasn't with you. (*She folds another napkin, nervously*)

Brian Jane Smith.

Sheila Exactly!

Brian In Florio's.

Sheila Yes. We're very old friends.

Brian And *you* had a lot to drink.

Sheila (*defensively*) We were celebrating! It was a school reunion.

Brian Only two of you left?

Sheila It was a very select school. Anyway, how did *you* know I was dining with Jane?

Brian Because it was Jane who asked me to join you for a drink.

Sheila And you . . . you *did*?

Brian Yes.

Sheila A glass of wine?

Brian Two or three, as a matter of fact.

Sheila Two or three?!

Brian (*with a shrug*) Three or four. I lost count. And so did *you*. I suppose that's why you . . . (*He peters out, leaving the unfinished sentence hanging in the air*)

Sheila Why I what?

Brian Well . . . said what you said . . . and did what you did.

Sheila looks at him for a moment in alarm. Then her good sense returns and she dismisses the idea. She escapes from him.

Sheila I don't believe a word of this! For a start, Jane has never even mentioned you to me. How long have you known her?

Brian Oh, not very long. We met a few weeks ago at a party at the press agency I work for, and I happened to recognize her in the restaurant on Friday.

Sheila Then you should have had the good manners to say a brief hallo and move on. There was no need to stop for a drink!

Brian No. But I'm jolly glad I did. (*He smiles his smile*)

Sheila W-what do you mean?

Brian Well, if I hadn't stopped for a drink I wouldn't have got to know *you*, and I wouldn't be here today.

Sheila (*out of her depth*) No, and I wish you weren't! Anyway, you can hardly call having a casual drink or two in a restaurant getting to *know* someone.

He smiles at her in disbelief.

Brian You *have* forgotten, haven't you?

Sheila W-what?

Brian Well . . . it wasn't just a drink or two in a restaurant, was it?

Sheila W-wasn't it?

Brian Oh, no! That was just the beginning.

Sheila What beginning?

Brian (*significantly*) I gave you a lift in my taxi . . .

Sheila Why?

Brian Because Jane was going in the opposite direction.

Sheila (*relieved*) Oh, I see! You took me to the station.

Brian N-no . . .

Sheila No?

Brian Not straight away . . .

Sheila (*apprehensively*) I beg your pardon?

Brian Well, you'd had quite a lot to drink . . .

Sheila Had I?

Brian Oh, yes. So . . . so I took you back to my flat.

Sheila tries to dismiss the idea.

Sheila Now you're just being silly!

Brian That wasn't what you said *then*.

Sheila Oh? What *did* I say?

Brian Well—*I* said would you like to come upstairs for a quick one and you said yes.

Sheila I *hope* I've misunderstood you!

Brian (*reassuringly*) So we went upstairs to my flat and I gave you a cup of black coffee. You *really* don't remember?

Sheila (*defiantly*) Of course I don't!

Brian Or are you just *pretending* not to?

Sheila avoids his eyes and moves away a little.

Sheila Why should I do that?

Brian Because you don't want to admit that it happened.

Sheila W-what happened?

Brian (*enigmatically*) The wine and the coffee . . . and everything.

Sheila I don't remember *any*thing, never mind *every*thing!

Brian Well, that's all right, then, isn't it? What you don't remember needn't worry you. Afterwards, you took a taxi to the station and got the last train back here.

Sheila Afterwards? How long did I stay in your flat? (*Hopefully*) Ten minutes?

Brian Oh, a bit longer than that . . .

Sheila A cup of coffee wouldn't take more than ten minutes, surely?

Brian About an hour and a half.

Sheila (*alarmed*) An hour and a half?! Oh, dear . . .!

Brian You needn't worry. I enjoyed myself enormously.

Sheila (*appalled*) For an hour and a half?

Brian Well, we did seem to get into the swing of it.

Sheila And then you put me into a taxi and sent me off to the station?

Brian I did ask you to stay.

Sheila cannot help being pleased.

Sheila Did you?

He looks at her, penetratingly.

Brian Oh, yes . . .
Sheila All night . . .?
Brian H'm. (*He sighs, regretfully*) But you said you had to go home.

The sensible married woman reasserts herself.

Sheila Well, of course I had to go home! What would Andrew have said if I'd stayed out all night?
Brian You could have missed your train.

Sheila sighs, almost regretfully.

Sheila I haven't missed my train for years . . . (*She quickly pulls herself together again*) You *are* making this up aren't you? I don't believe *any*thing happened!
Brian Don't you? Not *any*thing?

He smiles at her, enigmatically. Sheila holds his look for a moment, uncertain of the truth. He leans a little closer to her and speaks softly . . .

I don't suppose there's any chance of a cup of coffee . . .?
Sheila This is no time for coffee! (*She paces away, distractedly*)
Brian Gin and tonic?
Sheila Nothing!
Brian Oh, dear . . .
Sheila Whatever happened, you shouldn't have *let* it happen! What *did* happen?
Brian Oh, I couldn't tell you that. I'm far too much of a gentleman.
Sheila Not enough of a gentleman to keep away from my house!
Brian Well, it was your idea.
Sheila Was it?
Brian Yes, You said it would be quite convenient here, and that this Sunday would be a good day for it.
Sheila (*outraged*) I'm sure I never said that! (*Evasively*) I may have said—vaguely—you must come to lunch sometime. That's just good manners. I say that to everybody. But I don't expect to be taken seriously.
Brian I must have misunderstood. I thought you meant that we were going to carry on from where we left off.
Sheila Where we left off? (*Apprehensively*) Where *did* we leave off?
Brian (*smiling*) Can't you remember that, either?
Sheila (*nervously*) I—I don't know what you're talking about. (*She turns away towards the garden and sees someone outside*) Oh, good heavens!
Brian What's the matter?
Sheila How am I going to explain you away to my husband? (*She waves a hand towards the garden*)

It is Brian's turn to be alarmed. He goes across to her, quickly.

Brian Your husband?! You didn't tell me *he* was here!
Sheila He *lives* here!
Brian I know he lives here, but I didn't think he was going to *be* here!
Sheila Well, he *is* here!
Brian You said he was going to be away this weekend—on business!

Sheila He was. But his plans have changed and now he's out there in the garden with his boots on. He's a very keen gardener. Famous for his marrows.

Brian (*anxiously*) And now he's coming in *here*?

Sheila Well, he's been in the garden for two hours already, and he's got a very low threshold of boredom. Whatever's he going to think when he comes in and finds *you* here?

Brian I'm not waiting to find out! (*He starts to go*)

Sheila (*restraining him*) Where are you going? You can't just disappear!

Brian I thought you wanted me to?

Sheila I know I did. But Andrew may have seen you arriving!

Brian Well, now he can see me going! (*He tries to go*)

Sheila (*clinging on to his arm*) But he's a solicitor!

Brian What's that got to do with it?

Sheila Well, solicitors ask questions, don't they? If he saw you arriving and then comes in and finds that you've disappeared, he'll want to know who you were and what you were doing here! So what am I going to tell him?

Brian (*dithering*) *I* don't know! Tell him anything! Tell him . . . tell him I'm the window-cleaner! Or your brother, or your uncle or something! (*Desperately*) Just don't tell him the truth!

Andrew appears on the patio, coming in from the garden in his wellington boots. He is a pleasant, relaxed man of about fifty

Andrew Any sign of coffee?

Sheila (*turning to him rather abruptly*) Andrew, you haven't finished in the garden already?

Andrew (*looking somewhat surprised*) I usually come in at this time, don't I? Have a cup of coffee. It is eleven o'clock.

Sheila You shouldn't get so set in your ways!

Andrew I wouldn't call a cup of coffee at eleven getting into a rut exactly. (*He crosses towards the dining-table, starting to take off his sweater*)

Sheila Well, you didn't give me any warning to put the coffee on.

Andrew You don't usually need any warning. (*He starts to pull the sweater over his head*)

Sheila And you don't usually come in until half-*past* eleven!

Brian (*nervously*) I expect today he reached his threshold of boredom a bit sooner. (*He smiles*)

Andrew turns, his face appearing from inside his sweater, and sees Brian for the first time. He looks puzzled.

Andrew I beg your pardon?

Brian hastily stops smiling

Brian Oh—sorry. I musn't do that.

Andrew Do what?

Brian Smile. She doesn't like me to smile.

Andrew Doesn't she? (*To Sheila*) Don't you, darling?

Sheila Well, not all the time!

Andrew No. No, I suppose all the time would be a little tiresome. (*He puts* *his sweater down*) Not that I've got anything against smiling, mind you. I'm sure you've got a very nice smile, as smiles go. But all the time would be a *bit* excessive, I suppose. (*To Sheila*) I didn't know you had a visitor.

Brian Didn't you see me arriving?

Andrew Oh, no. I was far too busy gardening.

Brian gives Sheila a hard look. Andrew moves towards Brian, puzzled.

Andrew I'm sorry, I —er— I don't think we've been——

Sheila (*intervening quickly*) He's just leaving! He only popped in for a rest, and now he's leaving.

Andrew Oh, don't hurry on my account. I only came in for a cup of coffee.

Sheila I wish you'd use the kitchen door when you've been gardening. Your boots get so muddy.

Brian Yes. Aren't you going to take them off?

Andrew (*faintly surprised*) I beg your pardon?

Brian Your boots. We don't want you messing up the carpet, do we?

Andrew Ah—no—that would never do. I'll take them off. (*He sits on the sofa to take his boots off*)

Brian (*going to him quickly, anxious to please*) I'll help you!

Andrew (*a little surprised by the offer*) I have managed before.

Brian But you must be tired! It's eleven o'clock and you haven't had your coffee yet. Come on—I'll give you a hand! (*He kneels below the sofa to help Andrew with his boots*)

Andrew turns to look at Sheila, who is hovering nervously.

Andrew Is that all right with you, Sheila? If he helps me off with my boots.

Sheila I don't care *what* he does!

Andrew Provided he doesn't smile, eh?

Sheila avoids Andrew's eyes, and goes to fold another table napkin. Andrew notices the bunch of flowers on the table behind the sofa.

You haven't been buying flowers, have you, darling?

Sheila (*jumping nervously*) What?

Andrew We've got masses of them in the garden.

Sheila Oh—a man came to the door with them. I just couldn't get rid of him. (*She glares at Brian*)

Brian (*abruptly*) I say—your artichokes are enormous!

Andrew What?

Brian Artichokes.

Andrew Ah! You saw them?

Brian As I came round the back.

Andrew Not as big as last year.

Brian (*impressed*) Bigger than that last year? I find that hard to believe.

Andrew As big as my fist! (*He demonstrates*)

Brian Good heavens . . .! (*He is helping Andrew off with his boots*)

Andrew (*pleased*) You interested in gardening?

Brian Oh, yes.

Andrew Good. Good. We must have a long talk about it.

Brian (*losing heart*) Well—I haven't got a very *big* garden.
Andrew Small patch, eh?
Brian (*modestly*) Window box.
Andrew Can't grow many artichokes there, eh?

They enjoy the joke. Sheila does not. Brian puts Andrew's boots down and picks up a pair of shoes from behind the armchair.

Brian These your shoes?
Andrew Yes. Bit too big for you, eh, Sheila?

He and Brian enjoy this also. Brian brings the shoes to Andrew.

Thanks. Now, then—how about that coffee?
Sheila (*edgily*) Why do you keep on about coffee all the time?
Andrew Well, it's a bit tiring out there, you know. All that digging. (*To Brian*) Very heavy land here. A lot of clay. You get much clay in your window box?

They laugh together.

Hard work always makes you thirsty. (*He starts to put his shoes on*)
Brian (*helpfully*) I'll put the coffee on for you. (*He makes for the kitchen doors*)
Andrew No, no, my dear fellow. You don't have to do that.
Sheila He can if he wants to!
Andrew (*surprised*) What?
Sheila Well, it's not very difficult, is it?
Andrew No. No, I appreciate that. I'm sure he's capable of putting the coffee on. I just thought that perhaps you—or I—might be a bit more suitable. Living here and all that. Anyway, he doesn't know where the kitchen is.
Sheila It's through there! He'll easily recognize it! (*She tries to urge Brian towards the kitchen*)
Andrew (*puzzled by her behaviour*) Yes, darling. I'm sure he will. It *is* easily recognizable—cooker, fridge, all that sort of thing. Easily identifiable. As a kitchen. I just felt it would be better if one of *us*—being residents, as it were—might be a bit more suitable.
Brian It's no trouble. I love cooking.
Sheila (*relieved*) Thank God for that . . .!
Brian What?
Sheila You'll find the coffee next to the grinder.
Brian Right. I shan't be long. Through here?
Sheila Yes.
Brian Right. (*He starts to go*)

Sheila notices the bunch of flowers behind Andrew, grabs them up quickly and shoves them into Brian's hands.

He hastily hides them behind his back and disappears into the kitchen.

Sheila returns to Andrew, and tries to look relaxed.

Andrew Seems a very nice chap.
Sheila Yes.

Andrew Very helpful. Eager.
Sheila Yes.

Quite a pause. Andrew is browsing through the Sunday papers. Sheila retrieves the colour supplement and flips through it, nervously.

Andrew Does he do that a lot?
Sheila Do what?
Andrew Wander into strange houses and put the coffee on.
Sheila (*defensively*) He's only trying to help!
Andrew Yes. Yes, I appreciate that. He does seem *very* helpful. And I do think you ought to allow him to smile occasionally.
Sheila It was just that he kept *on* doing it. (*She perches, awkwardly, on the arm of the chair*)
Andrew Even when you didn't say anything funny?
Sheila Yes! (*She flips through the magazine, not seeing any of it*)
Andrew Got a happy disposition, I suppose.
Sheila He'd just come up from the station!
Andrew Oh, well that explains it. He'll be glad of a cup of coffee.
Sheila (*abruptly*) I expect he had one on the train!
Andrew Oh. Oh, well, that's all right, then. (*He puts down his newspaper and looks at her*) Er—Sheila . . .
Sheila Y-yes, darling?
Andrew Am I losing my memory?
Sheila What do you mean?
Andrew Well, I don't remember meeting —er——
Sheila Brian.
Andrew Is that his name?
Sheila Yes.
Andrew Well, I don't remember meeting Brian before.
Sheila No?
Andrew No. It's not like me. My memory's usually so good. Golf club, was it?
Sheila No. You've *never* met. (*She goes out on to the patio to get the coloured sun umbrella*)
Andrew Ah! Well, that explains it. I was beginning to think I was slipping.
Sheila Oh, no.
Andrew Oh, good. (*After a pause*) Well?

Sheila cannot hear him, so she comes inside with the sun umbrella.

Sheila What?
Andrew The coffee maker. Who is he?
Sheila Oh. Brian.
Andrew Yes. I know that's his name, but what's he doing here?
Sheila Why?
Andrew Well, being a solicitor I suppose I do have an enquiring mind. Have you known him very long?
Sheila (*a little too defensively*) No, of course not! I'd have told you, wouldn't I?

Andrew Not necessarily. There's a chap I've known for years who works on a farming magazine. Writes about pigfood. I've never mentioned him to *you*. Why are you being so secretive?

Sheila I'm not! (*She busies herself with the sun umbrella*)

Andrew Yes, you are. And mysterious.

Sheila I'm not at all mysterious!

Andrew All right, then. Tell me who he is.

Sheila glances, briefly, towards the kitchen and recalls Brian's suggestions.

Sheila Well, he's ... he's the window-cleaner.

Andrew What?! (*Laughing*) He doesn't *look* like a window-cleaner.

Sheila Doesn't he?

Andrew Well, he hasn't got his bucket with him! (*He laughs loudly*)

Sheila Ah—no. He's ... he's my brother!

Andrew looks at her in surprise and laughs again

Andrew You haven't *got* a brother!

Sheila Er ... haven't I?

Andrew Well, I think I'd have spotted him at our wedding! Sheila, are you feeling all right?

Sheila Yes—of course I am ...

Andrew Then why are you talking about window-cleaners and brothers when you haven't got either?

Sheila (*trying to salvage something*) Oh, I ... I didn't mean *my* brother!

Andrew Oh? Then whose brother?

Sheila Er ... *her* brother!

Andrew Whose brother?

Sheila *Jane's* brother!

Andrew Jane Smith? The one you were having dinner with on Friday evening?

Sheila Yes. That's when she introduced us.

Andrew Who?

Sheila Me and Brian.

Andrew You mean Brian was at the dinner, too? I thought it was an Old Girls' Reunion.

Sheila (*flustered*) Why do you keep asking so many questions?

The umbrella shoots up and she stands there, looking rather incongruous beneath it.

He ... he just happened to be passing.

Andrew Where on earth were you eating? The middle of Piccadilly Circus?

Sheila He ... he was looking for his sister.

Andrew His sister Jane?

Sheila Yes.

Andrew (*deep in thought*) It's a funny thing, you know ...

Sheila What is?

Andrew Well, I always thought Jane was an only child. She's never mentioned a brother to me. (*He delves into "The Observer"*)

Sheila Ah. No. She wouldn't.

Andrew Why not?

Sheila She doesn't know him very well.

Andrew Doesn't know her own brother?

Sheila Well . . . the family don't like to talk about him.

Andrew Why not? Seems a pleasant enough chap. You know, if you keep
that thing up in the house something dreadful will happen.

Sheila It already has . . . !

*She goes out with the umbrella, puts it into the table socket on the patio and
returns. Andrew is deep in thought.*

Andrew I can't understand how Jane doesn't know her own brother very
well . . .

Sheila is forced to improvise.

Sheila Well, because . . . he —er— he went off to . . . to Africa when he
was very young!

Andrew Africa?

Sheila Yes. Under a bit of a cloud.

Andrew Sounds more like a downpour. You mean he was in some sort of
financial trouble?

Sheila (*grateful for the suggestion*) Yes! Yes, exactly! (*Then losing heart*) I
think so . . . Anyhow, they don't like to talk about it! None of them. (*She
leans over the end of the sofa, urgently*) So whatever happens, Andrew—you
musn't talk about it!

Andrew is a little taken aback by her vehemence.

Andrew Good heavens . . . ! What on earth did he do?

Sheila Well, I couldn't ask her that, could I?

Andrew Ah. No. No, I suppose not. (*He returns to his newspaper*)

Sheila They like to keep it a secret.

Andrew I'm not surprised! Jane hasn't seen him for many years, then?

Sheila No.

Andrew And then suddenly—there he was walking past your table in the
restaurant?

Sheila Yes. So naturally Jane asked him to join us for a glass of wine.

Andrew Only *one* glass after all that time in Africa?

Sheila Well . . . one or two.

Andrew One or two?

Sheila Two or three.

Andrew I should jolly well hope so!

Sheila And then—off he went.

Andrew Back to Africa?

Sheila No. To Amersham.

Andrew And does he know that Jane's coming here to lunch?

Sheila (*in sudden alarm*) Oh, my God—no he doesn't! (*She turns away,
anxiously, thinking hard*)

Andrew Well, what's he doing here, then?

Sheila hesitates, but only for a second, then turns back to him.

Sheila Jane forgot to give him her address.
Andrew Oh, I see. (*After a pause*) But *you* didn't forget to give him yours?
Sheila He must have looked it up in the telephone book!
Andrew Why couldn't he look up Jane's in the telephone book?
Sheila Darling, there are hundreds of Smiths in the telephone book.
Andrew (*thoughtfully*) H'm. Lucky we're called Brown, then, isn't it? (*He looks at her, quizzically*)

Luckily for Sheila, at this moment Brian returns with a tray of coffee things.

Brian Here we are! I wasn't very long, was I?
Andrew It's very kind of you.
Brian Shall I be mother?
Andrew Why not? You seem to be doing everything else.

Brian organizes the coffee on the dining-table. Sheila goes to him, quickly, anxious to be rid of him.

Sheila You can leave it there if you're in a hurry to go.
Andrew He doesn't have to rush off. You haven't given him Jane's address yet.
Brian (*puzzled*) Jane's address?
Sheila (*abruptly*) You've forgotten the sugar!
Brian No, I haven't. It's here. Sugar, sir?
Andrew No, thank you, Brian.
Brian (*reacting to the use of his first name*) What?
Andrew That *is* your name, isn't it?
Brian Yes, but I didn't think you knew.
Andrew Sheila told me. It wasn't a secret, was it? (*He chuckles*)
Brian Oh, no. No. Sugar, Sheila?
Sheila No, thank you. (*She sits, nervously, with her coffee*)

Brian takes a cup of coffee and the plate of biscuits across to Andrew

Andrew (*taking the coffee*) Thanks.
Brian Biscuit, sir? (*He offers the biscuits*)
Andrew No, thanks.
Brian Biscuit, Sheila?
Sheila No, thanks.
Brian Biscuit, Brian? Oh, thanks. (*To Andrew, nervously*) Did she ... tell you anything else? Apart from my name, I mean.
Andrew Well ... no. Not really. (*He sips his coffee*)

Brian nibbles a biscuit, nervously.

Very nice coffee, Brian.
Brian Oh. Good. Thanks. (*He looks on for a moment as Andrew and Sheila silently sip their coffee*) I think *I'll* have a cup ... (*He starts for the coffee*)
Sheila (*abruptly*) Didn't you get one on the train?

Brian stops, poised, half-way to the coffee. Andrew looks surprised at Sheila's tone of voice.

Andrew He can have another one if he wants to. It's a long walk up that hill from the station. Go on, Brian—help yourself.

Brian Oh . . . thanks. (*He helps himself*)

Andrew Must have been quite a surprise for you, Brian, walking into that restaurant on Friday and seeing her sitting there. (*Meaning his sister*)

Brian exchanges a look of panic with Sheila.

Brian You—you *know* about that?

Andrew Oh, yes.

Sheila I was telling Andrew how you joined me and Jane for a glass of wine.

Andrew (*laughing*) Three or four, you said!

Brian I hope you didn't mind me having a few drinks with your wife?

Andrew Good heavens, no! Why should I mind? Anyone can drink as much as they like. Provided they don't come home singing. (*To Sheila*) You didn't come home singing, did you, darling? No, of course you didn't. I heard you fall over your slippers, but what you said wouldn't go very well to music. (*He chuckles*)

Sheila I didn't think you were awake.

Andrew I wasn't till you fell over your slippers. Well, Brian—how long is it since you last saw her?

Unseen by Andrew, Brian glances at Sheila nervously, thinking Andrew is referring to her when in fact he is referring to Brian's sister.

Brian I've *never* seen her! Not before Friday!

Andrew Don't be silly. You must have done.

Brian No! I promise you! It was the first time we'd ever met!

Andrew (*incredulously*) Really?

Sheila puts her coffee down and gets up, abruptly.

Sheila Andrew, isn't it time you went back into the garden?

Andrew (*surprised at her urgency*) I'm still having my half-past-elevenses.

Sheila Well, hurry up, then! The weeds must be growing like mad out there.

Andrew (*To Brian*) I naturally assumed you must have known her before you disappeared after your . . . trouble.

Brian looks at Sheila, then back at Andrew again, puzzled.

Brian What trouble?

Sheila Andrew . . . !

Andrew (*apologetically*) Yes, I know I promised not to mention it, and I realize, Brian, that it's none of my business, but—well, I am a solicitor, so perhaps you'd like to talk to me about it? I'm always delighted to give advice if it's wanted.

Sheila Brian! Would you go and peel some potatoes? (*She grabs Brian and propels him towards the kitchen*)

Brian I thought Mrs Garbut had done them?

Sheila Well, she didn't do enough! Off you go!

Andrew No, no! Brian's done too much already. I'm sure he works hard all week, so he deserves a peaceful Sunday here in Little Buckden.

Sheila sits down again.

(*to Brian*) I simply can't get over you never having seen her before. Presumably your family drifted apart when you were still a baby?

Brian (*totally confused*) What?

Andrew Well, I presume your parents separated when you were still very small?

Brian (*bemused*) My parents weren't separated.

Andrew Weren't they? Oh, dear. They're dead, then?

Brian Dead? No. They're living in Tunbridge Wells.

The doorbell goes. Nobody makes a move. Andrew sips his coffee, thoughtfully. Brian looks from one to the other to see who is going to answer the door. A pause. Nobody goes.

I . . . I think I heard a doorbell.

Andrew (*casually*) Yes. It's ours.

Sheila (*reluctant to leave*) I didn't hear anything.

The doorbell goes again. A pause. Again nobody makes a move.

Brian (*to Andrew*) I *think* it was a doorbell.

Andrew I *know* it was a doorbell.

Sheila You could have been mistaken!

Andrew Don't be silly, darling. We've had that doorbell for five years. I think I know the sound of it by now.

Again the doorbell.

Brian (*eager to please*) Shall *I* go?

Andrew No, no! You've done enough already.

Sheila He might *like* answering doorbells!

Andrew He's made the coffee. That's enough to be going on with.

Brian I don't mind. Really.

Andrew Nothing of the sort. Sheila will go. It's probably for her, anyway.

Sheila (*reluctantly*) Oh, all right . . . (*She gets up and goes to the archway*) But don't *talk* to each other while I'm away.

Andrew What?

Sheila (*with a bright smile*) I do so hate missing conversations.

She goes out to the hall

Andrew (*puzzled*) I wonder what's got into her today. She doesn't usually mind answering doors. (*He puts his coffee cup down on the tray, then turns to Brian*) When did you get back, then?

Brian Back?

Andrew From Africa.

Brian thinks deeply. He has no idea what Andrew is talking about.

Brian I beg your pardon?

Andrew (*realizing he has breached a confidence*) Ah! All right! Sorry. Quite understand. You don't want to talk about it. Right. (*He puts his arm cordially*

around Brian's shoulders and leads him to the sofa) Whatever you did,
it's *your* affair. I agree. But you've got to look ahead now. It's the future
that matters. And I'm just the sort of chap who might be able to help you.
Brian (*puzzled*) Really?
Andrew Oh, yes. People in my position—well, we can usually assist chaps
like you to get back on to the straight and narrow.
Brian Straight and narrow?
Andrew Yes. Look—now you're here, you'll stay to lunch, won't you?
Brian (*nervously*) Er—well, I'm not sure that that's a good idea . . .
Andrew Of course it is! You can't go rushing back to Amersham when she'll
soon be arriving.

A pause. Brian looks puzzled.

Brian *Who*'ll soon be arriving?
Andrew Didn't Sheila tell you?
Brian Tell me what?
Andrew Your sister's coming to lunch!
Brian (*completely bemused*) My . . . my sister?!
Andrew Yes.
Brian Coming to lunch *here*?
Andrew Yes.
Brian Good Lord! I haven't seen her for ages.
Andrew (*his smile fading*) What?
Brian She must have got the train down this morning. Fancy you knowing
my sister . . .
Andrew What train?
Brian From Scotland!
Andrew From Scotland?

Sheila comes hurtling back in a rush from the hall.

Sheila There was nobody there!
Andrew I'm not surprised. You took so long answering the door.
Sheila (*crossing briskly to Brian*) Come on, Brian! It's time you were on your
way to the station.

*To Andrew's astonishment, Sheila pulls Brian up from the sofa and propels
him towards the hall.*

Andrew He's not going.
Sheila Of course he's going! (*She urges him a bit more*)
Andrew I've asked him to stay to lunch.
Sheila What?!
Brian (*to Sheila*) Yes, he *has*.
Andrew Well, it seemed a bit silly him not staying when his sister's coming.
Sheila Ah. Yes . . .
Andrew Besides, there are one or two things he and I need to discuss. We're
going to have a good long talk about the future.
Sheila (*in a panic*) He can't stay to lunch!
Andrew What?

Sheila He was just going to leave when you came in from the garden with your boots on! You can't stay, can you, Brian?

Andrew Of course he can. He can pour the wine.

Sheila No, he can't!

Brian Well, I have done it before.

Andrew Good! That's settled, then. You're staying to lunch, I'm going to get on with the garden, and you're going to do some more potatoes. *(He starts to take off his shoes)*

Brian I can do the potatoes!

Sheila Oh, thank you, Brian.

Brian *(to Andrew)* See you later, then, sir.

Andrew Yes, rather!

Sheila *(to Brian, quietly)* I'll come with you and explain.

Brian What? *(As she glares at him)* Oh—right.

Brian stumbles, nervously, out into the kitchen.

Sheila is about to follow him.

Andrew Explain?

Sheila What?

Andrew What is there to explain?

Sheila How to do it.

Andrew Not very complicated, peeling a potato.

Sheila There's a lot more to do besides potatoes. *(She starts to go)*

Andrew He's a nice, helpful chap.

Sheila *(hesitating at the kitchen door)* Yes.

Andrew First my boots. Then coffee. Now the potatoes.

Sheila Yes . . .

Andrew Seems very keen to impress.

Sheila He's just got good manners, that's all.

She disappears into the kitchen.

Andrew goes to get his boots, returns to the sofa and prepares to put them on.

Carole appears out in the garden. She sees the open doors on the patio and comes, nervously, into the drawing-room. She is carrying a big suitcase and a handbag, and is obviously unfamiliar with the surroundings. Carole is a remarkably pretty girl of about twenty-five with a perky, appealing personality. She sees Andrew sitting on the sofa and smiles, delightedly.

Carole Hallo!

Andrew looks up from his boots and sees her. He smiles at her, pleasantly.

Andrew Good heavens! Carole! What are *you* doing here?

Carole I say—your artichokes are enormous!

Andrew Not as big as last year.

Carole Bigger than that last year?

Andrew As big as my fist! *(He demonstrates)*

Carole Good heavens . . .! (*She stands there smiling, suitcase in hand*) I rang
the bell but you didn't answer. So I walked around through the garden.
It's looking very nice.
Andrew Oh, good. I've been digging a bit this morning, as a matter of fact.
Carole I'm surprised you had time for digging *today*.
Andrew Ah—well, I didn't go to church, you see. (*He grins*)
Carole Anyway, knowing you, I expect you got everything ready last night.
Andrew (*puzzled*) Sorry?
Carole Shall I put it down?
Andrew H'm?
Carole My suitcase.
Andrew If you like.
Carole I'll put it up here, shall I?
Andrew (*disinterestedly*) Oh. All right.

She puts it down

Andrew Bit heavy, is it?
Carole (*with a smile*) Well, it's got everything I need, hasn't it? Is *your* suitcase
out in the hall?
Andrew My suitcase? Oh, no. Mine's upstairs. In my bedroom. That's where
I keep it.
Carole Oh, I see. You're going to bring it down later?
Andrew (*puzzled*) I hadn't really thought of that . . . (*He cannot understand
what she is doing here*) Did I . . . did I forget to sign some letters, or some-
thing?
Carole Oh, no. You signed everything at work before you went to the office
party.
Andrew Oh, good. I just wondered.
Carole (*chattily*) Any chance of a cup of coffee?
Andrew You didn't get one on the train, then?
Carole (*slightly taken aback*) Well, I . . . I didn't think about it. Haven't you
got any?
Andrew Oh, yes. We've got plenty. Packets and packets of it. Like living
in Brazil! Get you some in a minute.
Carole (*looking out into the garden*) Ooh! It's such a lovely day! Aren't we
lucky?
Andrew (*looking up from his boots*) H'm?
Carole With the weather. I mean, it might have been stormy today, mightn't
it?
Andrew (*with a grin*) I wouldn't have done any digging then! It's very nice
of you to pop in, Carole. On your way somewhere, were you? Thought
you'd look in and say hallo.

Carole smiles at him, and shakes her head in playful disapproval.

Carole You're always joking, aren't you?
Andrew Joking?
Carole I *had* to come here first, didn't I?
Andrew Did you?

Carole Well, that's what we arranged!

Andrew (*surprised*) For you to come to Little Buckden?

Carole Yes, of course! Well, you're so close to the airport, aren't you?

Andrew Airport? Oh, yes. A few miles down the road. Gets a bit noisy in the summertime. (*He chuckles*)

Carole sees the coffee things, puts down her handbag and goes to the coffee.

Carole There's some over here!

Andrew What?

Carole Coffee. I say—there are a lot of cups. Have you had visitors?

Andrew Yes. As a matter of fact someone did pop in ... That'll be cold by now. We'll make you some fresh in a minute. Where are you off to, then?

She smiles, patiently, and gives him a playful push, which surprises him a little.

Carole Oh, come on! You haven't forgotten the itinerary, surely?

Andrew (*blankly*) Itinerary?

Carole We start at the Colosseum ...

Andrew The Colosseum? That little Italian restaurant just down the road? Pasta, all that sort of thing.

Carole (*giggling*) Don't be daft! The place. In Rome.

Andrew Oh, you mean the —er— *actual* ...?

Carole Yes, of course! (*Then, uncertainly*) It *is* in Rome, isn't it?

Andrew Oh, yes. It's in Rome all right. I see! So you're on your way to the airport?

Carole Of course! That's why I've got my suitcase! (*She smiles, happily*)

Andrew I did wonder ... (*He goes to put his shoes out of the way behind the armchair*) Well, I'm sure you'll find it all very interesting.

Carole You know, I can't get over you bothering with the garden. Today of all days. It's rather sweet. I suppose you like to leave everything tidy.

Andrew (*returning*) Well, you know how it is with garden rubbish Carole. Leave it a couple of weeks, get a drop of rain and it all goes black and messy. So I had a good big bonfire.

Carole Your wife will be pleased.

Andrew I don't suppose she'll notice. Sheila's not too interested in bonfires. Edges of the grass. Bit of pruning. That's more in her line.

Carole (*moving to him, a little fearfully*) Here—she doesn't suspect, does she?

Andrew (*chuckling*) She wouldn't be interested.

Carole She would if she found out!

Andrew No. Wouldn't make any difference. (*With a laugh*) I don't tell her every time I do it, you know.

Carole You mean you've done it before?

Andrew Good Lord, yes! I like to do it once a week if I get the chance.

Carole (*far from pleased*) Once a week? You never told me that!

Andrew cannot understand her fascination with bonfires.

Andrew Well, it's not the sort of thing that crops up when I'm dictating a letter to a client. "Dear Sir, further to your letter of the twelfth instant, Oh, by the way, I had a bonfire today."

Carole We weren't talking about bonfires!

Andrew Weren't we?

Carole I meant—are you sure she doesn't know about *me*?

Andrew Oh. No, I don't think so. I don't think I've ever mentioned you to her. After all, you haven't been working in my office very long, have you? (*He has a sudden idea*) Look—you're not dashing off for a minute, are you?

Carole Of course I'm not dashing off . . .

Andrew Oh, good! I'll just go and get Sheila to come and say hallo to you, then. She'd like to meet you. (*He starts for the kitchen*)

Carole (*alarmed*) Sheila? Is your wife *here*, then?

Andrew She *lives* here!

Carole Yes, I know she lives here. But I didn't think she was going to *be* here!

Andrew Well, she *is* here. She's in the kitchen. With Brian. They're getting the lunch ready. Sunday, you see. Roast beef and Yorkshire pudding. Kind of a tradition in this house.

Carole (*puzzled*) Who's Brian?

Andrew I'm not quite sure . . . Hang on a minute! I'll go and get Sheila. (*He starts to go again*)

Carole But won't she wonder what I came here for?

Andrew (*stopping and turning*) Yes. I suppose she will. What *did* you come here for?

Carole Well—to meet *you*, of course! So we could go on to the airport *together*.

Andrew You and me?

Carole (*impatiently*) Don't say you've forgotten? It's today that we're going to Italy together!

A pause. Andrew stares at her, blankly.

Andrew Sorry?

Carole (*romantically*) You said you wanted to go to all the beautiful places in the world and see them with somebody special. That's *me*!

Andrew moves to her, considering this.

Andrew Did *I* say that?

Carole You certainly did!

Andrew It . . . it doesn't sound quite like me, somehow, *When* did I say that?

Carole On Friday at the office party.

Andrew (*relieved*) Ah! Well, that explains it! People say a lot of things they don't mean at office parties. Funny things happen to people at office parties. They do tend to exaggerate.

Carole That's what *I* said.

Andrew When?

Carole On Friday at the office party.

Andrew Well, there you are, then! (*He chuckles*)

Carole But you said, "No, I'm a solicitor and my word is my bond."

Andrew (*dumbfounded*) I didn't say that!

Carole You certainly did! We made a date there and then. I wrote it down in my diary.

Andrew Do you *always* take your diary to office parties?

Carole Well, I don't want to forget what I'm told, do I?

Andrew Secretaries get told lots of things at office parties. They're not supposed to remember them the next day!

Carole Then you shouldn't say them, should you? So here I am—all packed up and ready to go!

Andrew, his peaceful Sunday in tatters, considers his campaign. He glances, anxiously, towards the kitchen, and then sits next to her and speaks, confidentially.

Andrew Look ... er ... Carole—I think there has been a—how can I put this?—a slight misunderstanding here and——

Carole There's no misunderstanding. You asked me to go away with you, and I said yes. If you don't mean things you shouldn't say them. You're old enough to know better.

Andrew considers for a moment.

Andrew Perhaps I can explain this another way ... You see, the thing is, Carole—I've been in the garden for a time—about two hours, as a matter of fact—and I was going to have lunch, you see. That is, my wife and I——

Carole And Brian.

Andrew And Brian, yes. We were going to have lunch. Roast beef and Yorkshire pudding. All that sort of thing. So—it is a *little* difficult—at this particular time—to change the plans, as it were. So the best thing—and I'm sure you'll agree—is if I get the car out, and we'll have you back on the train in ten minutes. (*He starts to take his boots off again*)

Carole No.

Andrew Ah. I was hoping for an affirmative.

Carole You could hardly have expected one.

Andrew No. No, possibly not. But ... er ... you must see, it would be very difficult—in my present position—to give up——

Carole Roast beef and Yorkshire pudding.

Andrew Roast beef and——No! Not just that. To pack up and go flying off somewhere just because of something I said—in my cups—during the office party on Friday.

Carole (*sweetly reasonable*) Well, if it's Sunday lunch you're worrying about the flight doesn't go until three-fifteen. I can wait.

Andrew Yes. Well, that's very nice of you, Carole. Very nice indeed. And please don't think that I don't appreciate it. I do. It's just that, with the best will in the world, I *do* feel that Rome is just a little too far to go after roast beef and Yorkshire pudding.

Carole Oh, I see! You don't want to travel on a full stomach! Well, don't have it, then. (*She gets up*)

Andrew But I'm hungry!

Carole Don't you worry, darling. We'll get something on the plane. (*She goes to get her handbag*)

Andrew (*desperately*) Carole—my *wife* is out there in the kitchen!
Carole That doesn't matter. You can tell her it's a business trip.
Andrew But I'm not going anywhere!
Carole (*firmly*) Oh, yes, you *are*!

Andrew thinks of a way out and follows her in his socks.

Andrew Ah! Wait a minute! I've just thought of something. We can't go to
Italy anyway.
Carole Why not?
Andrew Because the planes are all full at this time of the year—(*triumphantly*)
and *I* didn't book any tickets!
Carole No—but *I* did!
Andrew What?!
Carole I booked them Club Class on the office account. I'm not your efficient
secretary for nothing. (*She produces two air tickets from her handbag and
thrusts them into his hands*)
Sheila (*off*) Andrew! Andrew!

Andrew quickly hides the air tickets under a magazine as . . .

Sheila comes in from the garden.

Have you seen Brian anywhere?
Andrew I thought he was in the kitchen.
Sheila No. When I got out there he'd disappeared. I've been looking for him
everywhere.
Andrew (*flustered*) Well, *I* dunno—perhaps he went home—decided not to
stay for lunch, after all.
Sheila Oh, I do hope so . . .! Why have you taken your shoes off?
Andrew (*fed up*) I'm just putting them on! (*He stomps away to look for his
shoes*)

Sheila sees Carole for the first time. She has no idea who she is.

Sheila Oh. Hallo . . . (*She looks back at Andrew and sees him on all fours*)
Andrew . . .? What *are* you doing?
Andrew I'm looking for my shoes!

Sheila smiles at Carole, embarrassed, and goes to Andrew, urgently.

Sheila Andrew! Andrew—aren't you going to introduce us?
Andrew (*looking up from the floor*) Oh. Yes. This is my wife.
Sheila (*whispering urgently*) Andrew! I know who *I* am; I want to know who
she is!
Andrew (*whispering also*) I . . . I don't know . . .!
Sheila What?
Andrew She . . . er . . . she just came in from the garden. (*He crawls off
behind the armchair, looking for his shoes*)

Sheila goes to Carole, wearing the smile of the polite hostess.

Sheila Ah! So it was *you* who rang the doorbell!
Carole (*nervously*) Yes. I'm ever so sorry . . .

Sheila Andrew really is dreadful. He simply refused to answer it. (*She returns to Andrew*) Andrew . . .?

Andrew looks out from behind the armchair.

Andrew I think she wanted to look at the garden. (*He disappears again*)

Sheila (*crossing back to Carole with a big smile*) Oh, I see! You're interested in gardens?

Carole (*uncertainly*) Well, I . . . I quite like looking at them, I suppose.

Sheila (*smiling graciously*) How nice.

Carole Yours is lovely. You must be a very good gardener.

Sheila Oh, no. Andrew's the expert. All *I* can manage is a little cress on a facecloth. (*She looks back at the armchair*) Andrew!

He appears over the back of the armchair with his shoes.

Andrew! Will you stop hiding in your shoes!

Andrew What?

Sheila (*quietly*) Who is she?

Andrew (*whispering urgently*) *I* don't know! She just seems to enjoy looking at flowers. Nothing wrong in that, is there?

Sheila But our garden isn't open to the public.

Andrew Well, I expect she thought it was! (*He sits in the armchair to put his shoes on*)

Sheila (*turning to Carole*) Don't you have a garden of your own?

Carole No. I live in a flat. I don't *want* a garden.

Sheila You mean you prefer looking at other people's?

Carole (*bewildered*) Well . . .

Andrew (*busy with his shoes*) I shan't be a minute . . .

Sheila (*politely*) I'm *so* sorry I wasn't here when you arrived. I was out in the kitchen.

Carole Yes, I know. With Brian.

Sheila (*surprised*) You *know* about Brian?

Carole I know he was in the kitchen.

Sheila looks at Andrew. He smiles, sheepishly.

Andrew It came out in the conversation.

Sheila Yes. I'm sure it did. "My hollyhocks are doing awfully well this year and Brian's in the kitchen"!

Andrew It wasn't like that!

Sheila Wasn't it?

Andrew No. We never even mentioned hollyhocks.

Carole (*to Sheila*) I hope you didn't mind me looking at your garden.

Sheila Of course not. I'm delighted. As long as you don't tell all your friends about it. We don't want hordes of people peering at the petunias. Not unless they've paid, of course! Do you know his *second* name?

Carole Whose second name?

Sheila Brian's.

Carole Oh. No.

Sheila Neither do I . . . (*She glances towards the garden, thoughtfully*)

Andrew (*getting up, abruptly*) Right! I've got my shoes on. Now I'll run you down to the station. (*He goes to Carole, urgently*)

Carole I'm not going to the station!

Andrew Oh, yes, you are . . .!

Sheila (*to Carole*) Have you had any coffee?

Carole It was cold!

Sheila I'll make you some fresh.

Andrew She hasn't time for coffee! She's got a train to catch.

Carole No, I haven't . . .!

Sheila Oh, dear. The trains are rather desultory in Little Buckden on a Sunday.

Andrew Right! I'll get the car out! (*He starts to go towards the garden, dragging Carole with him*)

Carole You needn't bother!

Andrew I *want* to! I want to drive you to the station!

Sheila You make her sound like a flock of sheep.

Andrew Come on! If we're quick we'll just catch the twelve-fifteen.

He drags Carole, protesting, out into the garden.

Sheila watches them go, puzzled, then crosses to look out of the other window, anxiously.

Brian comes in from the kitchen, excitedly.

Brian Sheila!

Sheila (*jumping*) Ah—you're still here, then?

Brian Of course I'm still here. I say—I think she's arrived!

Sheila Who?

Brian My sister! (*He heads for the garden*)

Sheila Brian!

Brian (*stopping*) What?

Sheila (*going to him, urgently*) I couldn't find you anywhere! Andrew thought you might have gone home.

Brian Don't be silly. How can I go home when my sister's coming to lunch? (*He starts to go again*)

Sheila Brian!

He stops.

Sheila I wanted to speak to you but you'd disappeared!

Brian I only went into the garden.

Sheila You said you'd be in the kitchen.

Brian I was trying to be helpful. I knew you'd want some mint for the potatoes.

Sheila (*exasperated*) You didn't have to take all day!

Brian I couldn't find it, anyway. It's a hell of a big garden, isn't it? I was wandering about for hours. Do *you* know where he hides the stuff?

Sheila (*trying to be patient*) Brian, there's something more important that I want to talk to you about. (*She takes his arm and leads him away, conspiratorially*)

Brian Can't it wait? She's out there and I want to say hallo! (*He tries to go again*)

Sheila That girl is of no importance!

Brian What?!

Sheila Now, look—in order to avoid any embarrassment—I have had to tell Andrew certain things, and I'd be grateful if——

Brian No importance? My sister?

Sheila (*stopped in full flow*) What?

Brian Out there in the garden with Andrew!

Sheila She's not your sister.

Brian Isn't she?

Sheila No, of course not.

Brian Then who *is* she?

Sheila (*uninterestedly*) I've no idea. Just some strange girl who seems to be going around looking at people's gardens. Now, look—the thing is——

Brian Didn't she introduce herself?

Sheila No, she didn't!

Brian Then she *might* be my sister!

Sheila Brian, she is not your sister!! In fact, that's what I wanted to talk to you about——

Brian I say, I hope she'll recognize me. I haven't seen her for years, you know. She spent a lot of time in Australia before she went to live in Scotland.

Sheila Who did?

Brian My sister!

Sheila (*desperately*) Will you please listen!

Brian It's jolly nice of you to invite her. I didn't even know you *knew* my sister. Where did you meet her?

Sheila (*loudly*) Brian!!

Andrew walks in from the hall.

Andrew Sorry about that.

Sheila You were very quick! You must have driven awfully fast.

Andrew Oh, no. She wouldn't let me take her in the car. Went dashing off before I could stop her.

Sheila (*innocently*) Oh, dear. Perhaps something upset her. So how is she getting to the station? Don't say she's going on foot?

Andrew Why not? It's downhill all the way. The rate she was going she'll be half-way there by now.

Sheila (*moving away*) Oh, well, I suppose she can always look at some more gardens on the way.

Andrew (*quietly*) Anyway, she's gone, that's the main thing ...

Brian (*to Andrew*) You know, I thought that girl might have been my sister.

Andrew Don't be ridiculous. I know what your sister looks like.

Brian *Do* you?

Andrew Of course!

Brian Well, that's more than I do!

Andrew gazes at him in astonishment.

Sheila (*puzzled*) Andrew ...

Andrew Yes?

Sheila Are you *going* somewhere?

Andrew Well, I may go back in the garden in a minute. Once I've got my boots on again.

Sheila I mean, you're not intending to travel anywhere?

Andrew (*over-reacting*) No!!

Sheila looks astonished at his vehemence.

Sheila What?

Andrew (*more quietly*) I mean—no, of course not, darling. Why should I be travelling anywhere?

Sheila That's what I thought. You cancelled your business trip this weekend, didn't you? But there's a suitcase up here . . .

Andrew (*nervously*) W-what?

Sheila brings Carole's suitcase down to him. He regards it, impassively, for a moment.

Yes . . . yes, that's a suitcase all right. But it's not mine!

Sheila Isn't it? (*She looks more closely*) Oh, no, it's not, is it, darling? More like a *lady*'s suitcase . . .

Andrew Ah. Yes. (*Suddenly*) It's probably Mrs Garbut's.

Sheila Why should Mrs Garbut bring a suitcase when she comes to clean?

Andrew (*hopefully*) Dusters?

Sheila Don't be silly, Andrew! Cleaning ladies don't arrive with suitcases.

Andrew It must be yours, then!

Sheila (*patiently*) Andrew, I do know what my own suitcases look like.

Andrew (*with sudden inspiration*) I know! Brian's sister! She's bound to have some luggage.

Brian She hasn't got here yet.

Andrew Luggage in advance?

Sheila Ah! Maybe it belongs to that girl?

Andrew (*apprehensively*) W-what girl?

Sheila The Garden Wanderer.

Andrew Why should *she* be carrying a suitcase?

Sheila I don't know, darling, but if it doesn't belong to anyone else it *must* be hers. (*She puts the suitcase on the end of the sofa*) We'll open it up and have a look inside. There's bound to be a name and address. (*She tries to open the suitcase*)

Andrew You can't do that!

Sheila Why not?

Andrew It'll be locked!

Sheila Yes. It is. Never mind. I shall take it into the kitchen and force it with a skewer. (*She starts to go, carrying the suitcase*)

Andrew You will not!

He restrains her, and they grapple with the suitcase.

Sheila Darling, I'm only going to ease it. We've got to find out where she lives, haven't we?

Andrew Well . . . yes, I suppose so, but——

Sheila And there's only one way to do that. The kitchen skewer!

She wins the battle for the suitcase, banging his knee in the process, and heads majestically for the kitchen. Andrew follows her, rubbing his knee.

Andrew No! Look—wait a minute! Sheila! Sheila! You can't go tampering with other people's property!

He goes out after Sheila into the kitchen, closing the door after him.

Brian watches them go, amused, and then starts to tidy up the coffee things on the dining-table.

Carole comes in from the garden.

Carole Hallo . . .

He turns and sees her.

Brian Ah—you didn't go to the station, then?

Carole Not likely! I didn't come all the way here just to go back to the station! (*She peers at him*) I suppose you must be *Brian*?

Brian (*his eyes lighting up*) Yes! Yes, I am!

Carole I thought you might be . . .

Brian jumps to the wrong conclusion and smiles delightedly.

Brian I knew I was right! It *is* you, isn't it? It really *is* you! And they were sending you away! You must have thought them awfully rude. They didn't realize, you see. Oh, it's *wonderful* to see you again!

Carole (*a little taken aback*) What?

Brian This *is* exciting, isn't it?

Carole Is it?

Brian I wasn't sure what time you'd be arriving. It's all been kept a bit of a secret. If I'd known I'd have met the train. Well, I never! Let's have a look at you!

Carole What?!

Brian Go on—turn around! Let's have a good look.

Puzzled, Carole slowly revolves for his inspection.

Well, well! You've certainly grown up into a pretty little thing.

Carole (*bemused*) Oh. Thanks very much. (*She moves away a little, thoughtfully*).

Brian (*grinning*) Your teeth all fell into the right places, then?

Carole Well, I don't have any difficulty eating . . .

Brian (*chuckling, happily*) Aah! You always did have a wonderful sense of humour! You know, I'd never have recognized you. Of course, it was a long time ago, wasn't it?

Carole I'm sorry. I don't quite . . .

Brian goes to her and holds out his arms, invitingly.

Brian Well—come on, then!

Carole What?

Brian Aren't you going to give me a hug?

Astonished, she retreats a little.

Carole Do you behave like this with *every* strange girl you meet?

Brian (*laughing*) Don't be daft! You're not a strange girl. You're my sister.

Carole (*puzzled*) What?!

Brian You've just arrived from Scotland.

Carole I've never ever *been* to Scotland.

Brian Don't you live in Inverness?

Carole No. I live in Bayswater.

Brian Well, *I* didn't know that. Why didn't you send me a change of address card?

Carole What *are* you talking about?

Brian parades a little, showing himself off.

Brian Well? Would *you* have recognized *me*? (*He grins, idiotically*)

Carole How could I? I've never seen you before!

Brian Never seen me? (*He laughs, noisily*) Come off it! I'm your brother!

Carole I haven't got a brother!

He gazes at her in disbelief for a moment.

Brian You . . . you haven't?

Carole No.

Brian But I thought you were my sister coming here for lunch.

Carole No, of course not!

Brian (*feeling rather ridiculous*) I'm so sorry. I thought you were—you must have thought I was an idiot!

Carole Yes. I did. (*She goes to where she left her suitcase and sees that it has gone*) What's happened to my suitcase?

Brian Ah! So it *does* belong to you?

Carole Of course it does. Where is it?

Brian It's in the kitchen.

Carole (*surprised*) What?

Brian Sheila took it there. She's trying to open it with a skewer.

Carole Open my suitcase? Whatever for?

Brian To find your name and address. (*Puzzled*) Wait a minute, though—I don't understand. If you just came here to look at the garden, why on earth were you carrying a suitcase?

Carole (*laughing*) Oh, I'm not just here to look at the garden . . .

Brian Then what are you here for?

Carole (*joyfully conspiratorial*) S'sh! I'm on my way . . . to Italy! (*She smiles, happily*)

Brian Really? I didn't know you checked in for Naples at Little Buckden! (*He laughs*) Why didn't you go straight to the airport? It's only a few miles down the road. Why stop off here?

Carole Well, I'm not going *alone*, am I?

Brian I should hope not! Pretty little thing like you. Couldn't possibly go alone. You know what those Italians are like. All pasta and pinching. You'd be black and blue in no time.

Carole So we arranged to meet here.

Brian In Little Buckden?

Carole Yes.

Brian You and your feller?

Carole Yes.

Brian Why?

Carole Well, he *lives* here, doesn't he?

Brian In Little Buckden?

Carole Yes.

Brian Oh, I see! And you'd forgotten his address?

Carole What?

Brian That's why you wandered in here.

Carole Oh, no! You see, he lives—— (*She stops herself just in time*)

But Brian jumps to the correct conclusion all the same.

Brian Lives *here*? You don't mean you're going with ...? (*He beams with joy at the thought*) Not with *him*? With old Andrew? Good Lord ...!

Sheila comes sailing in from the kitchen with the suitcase.

Sheila It's no good. I couldn't do it without—— (*She sees Carole*) Oh! I thought you'd gone. (*She tries to hide the suitcase behind her legs*)

Brian She forgot her suitcase.

Sheila So it *was* yours?

Carole Yes ...

Sheila Oh, good!

Carole The skewer didn't work, then?

Sheila (*innocently*) Skewer?

Carole To open the suitcase.

Sheila darts a glance at Brian.

Sheila I'm sure I don't know what you're talking about.

Carole Isn't that what you said she was doing, Brian?

Sheila (*to Brian, coldly*) You *have* been having a nice little chat, haven't you?

Brian (*grinning, affably*) I was only being sociable. Trying to keep the conversation going.

Sheila Well, you seem to have succeeded.

Brian Yes, I certainly have! (*He grins at Carole*)

Sheila (*to Carole*) We didn't know whose case it was, you see, and we thought there might be a name and address inside.

Carole Can I have it back, then?

Sheila What? Oh, yes, of course. Here you are.

She hands the suitcase to Carole, who puts it down beside her

And I'm sorry you had all the trouble of coming back to collect it. Brian, would you go and ask Andrew to get the car out? (*Moving away to check the dining-table*) Then he can take this young lady back to the station.

Carole I'm not going to the——

Brian I've got a *much* better idea! (*He smiles in anticipation*)
Sheila (*warily*) Have you?
Brian Why don't you ask her to stay to lunch?

Sheila is far from pleased, but does her best to retain her good manners.

Sheila Lunch? Oh. Well, I . . .
Brian She must be jolly hungry by now.
Sheila Possibly, but I'm sure she doesn't want to stay *here* for lunch . . .
Brian Of course she does! (*To Carole*) You do, don't you?
Carole No! I'm supposed to be going to——!

Andrew walks in from the kitchen.

Andrew Who's hidden the bottle opener? I can't find it anywhere. (*He sees Carole*) What the hell have *you* come back for?
Sheila (*appalled at his manners*) Andrew!
Brian (*with heavy innuendo*) She came to get her suitcase . . .

Andrew overdoes his surprise.

Andrew Oh, it was *yours*? Ah—well. We were all puzzled, you see. Couldn't identify it. None of us. And it was yours all the time. Well, well, well!
Carole But you *knew* it was mine.

Sheila looks at Andrew, puzzled.

Sheila *Did* you, Andrew?
Andrew Of course I didn't! How could I possibly have known that?
Sheila Well, you *were* here when she arrived.
Brian Yes, and presumably she was carrying it then.
Andrew No, she wasn't!
Carole Yes, I was.
Brian There you are, you see? She was.
Andrew Were you?
Carole Don't you remember?
Andrew Well, I . . . er . . .
Brian Surely you must have noticed that she was carrying a suitcase?
Andrew I noticed she was carrying *some*thing. I can't remember it being a suitcase, though.
Brian What did you think it was? The garden roller?
Andrew (*to Carole*) Anyway, you've got it back so there's no point in lingering. I'll get the car out and run you down to the station. (*He starts to go*)
Brian But she's not going to the station.
Andrew Of course she's going to the station! When you leave somewhere you always go to the station.
Brian But she's *not* leaving somewhere.
Andrew Yes, she is. She's leaving here.
Brian No, she's not. She's staying to lunch.
Andrew She is *not*!!

They all look at Andrew surprised at his outburst.

Sheila Andrew . . . !

Andrew Well . . . there isn't any room.

Brian We can *make* room, can't we? She can squeeze in next to you. You wouldn't mind that, would you?

Andrew is puzzled by Brian's innuendoes.

Andrew (*desperately*) But she can't stay to lunch! (*Going to Carole*) You can't stay to lunch, can you, Carole?

Sheila Carole? Is that her name?

Andrew Isn't it?

Carole Yes. It is.

Andrew (*to Sheila*) There you are—yes, it is!

Sheila I just didn't think it had been mentioned, that's all.

Andrew Of course it's been mentioned. I wouldn't have known it if it hadn't been mentioned, would I? She mentioned it when she first arrived. I remember.

Brian Ah! You remembered her name but not her suitcase?

Andrew crosses to Brian, glaring at him.

Andrew She can't stay to lunch!

Brian Yes, she can. She'd love to. You'd love to, wouldn't you, Carole?

Carole No!

Brian (*to Andrew*) Yes, she'd love to.

Sheila And then after lunch she can go and look at some more *wonderful* gardens.

But Carole has reached the end of her tether.

Carole I wish you'd stop going on about gardens! I don't like gardens!

They all look at her in surprise. Andrew panics immediately.

Andrew Of course you do! You love gardens! You said so!

Carole No, I didn't. I can't stand them!

Sheila Well, if you don't like gardens what on earth are you doing spending valuable time wandering about looking at them?

Carole But I wasn't looking at gardens!

Andrew wishes he was dead.

Sheila Then what *were* you doing?

Andrew crosses quickly to Sheila, almost tripping over the suitcase as he goes.

Andrew (*wildly*) She doesn't have to tell you that! (*To Carole*) You don't have to tell them that! (*To Sheila*) Will you stop asking questions all the time? What she was doing was her own affair!

Sheila Andrew, there is no need to get excited.

Andrew I just think it's very unfair to ask people a lot of questions the minute they enter your house. When your aunt came from Sidlesham to visit us I didn't ask her why she arrived with three suitcases and a carrier bag.

Sheila She was coming for Christmas.

Andrew The point is I didn't go on and on about her luggage.

Sheila I really don't see the harm in Carole telling us what she was doing here. Do you, Brian?

Brian No. I think it would be rather fun to know!

He grins at Carole, who looks somewhat apprehensive. Sheila goes to Carole.

Sheila Well, Carole—what *were* you doing here?

Hastily, Andrew tries to save the day.

Andrew Boy Scouts!

They all look at him in surprise.

Sheila Boy Scouts?

Andrew does a Boy Scout salute. Brian laughs at the spectacle.

Andrew You know what Boy Scouts are. Funny hats, toggles, that sort of
thing.

Sheila Yes. I know what Boy Scouts are. It's just that looking at Carole,
Boy Scouts don't immediately spring to mind. Carole dear, I know you'll
think I'm being frightfully silly, but what exactly were you *doing* with the
Boy Scouts in Little Buckden?

Carole Well, actually, I——

Andrew Collecting things! She was collecting things. For their jumble sale.
It's next week. And that's why she was carrying a suitcase.

Sheila turns to Carole, deeply impressed by her public-spiritedness.

Sheila You mean your suitcase is full of jumble?

Andrew Yes, of course it is!

Sheila I was asking Carole. Well, Carole?

*A breathless moment for Andrew. He looks at Carole, helplessly. She decides
to let him off the hook.*

Carole Yes, of course it is.

Andrew sighs with relief. Brian looks at Carole in mock surprise.

Brian What? No pretty little dresses, brief bikinis, naughty nighties . . .?

Carole (*firmly*) No! (*She avoids his eyes*)

Brian Oh, dear. What a pity.

Sheila It's not a pity at all, Brian. Carole is doing wonderful things for the
Boy Scouts.

The doorbell goes.

Andrew Ah! That'll be Jane.

Sheila (*unconcerned*) Oh, no. It's far too early for Jane. (*She turns to Carole*)

Brian (*puzzled*) Jane? I didn't know *she* was coming, too . . .

Sheila Do you live in Little Buckden, then?

Carole Oh, no. I live in Bayswater.

Sheila *Bayswater*?

Brian crosses to Andrew, with a twinkle in his eyes.

Brian Good heavens! Isn't that wonderful, Andrew? What a sweet, kind girl to come all the way from London to help with a jumble sale in Little Buckden. (*He grins at Andrew*)

Andrew gives him a funny look, puzzled by his manner. The doorbell goes again.

Carole (*to Andrew*) I think I heard a doorbell.
Andrew Yes. It's ours.
Carole Doesn't anyone *ever* answer doorbells in this house?
Sheila I did it last time. It's Andrew's turn.
Andrew Oh, very well. (*He heads for the hall, relieved to have got over the immediate crisis*)
Brian Andrew . . .
Andrew (*turning*) Well?
Brian (*quietly*) That was a close one, wasn't it?
Andrew What?

Brian grins, knowingly.

Andrew gives him a doubtful look and goes out into the hall.

Sheila turns to Carole, enthusiastically.

Sheila Well, this *is* exciting! I simply adore jumble sales, don't you? And I can't understand how I didn't know about this one. (*Then aside to Brian*) Brian, I *must* talk to you! There's something you don't know . . .!
Brian And there's something *you* don't know, too . . .!

Sheila looks puzzled for a second, then turns back to Carole, trying to keep up appearances in front of a stranger.

Sheila You know, Andrew has got a really hideous sports jacket and some dreadful ties that I'm sure you can have.
Carole (*nervously*) Well, I think I've got enough already . . . (*She edges away with her suitcase*)
Sheila You can never have enough on these occasions. I've run jumble sales myself, and I know that enough is never enough! (*To Brian, urgently*) It's about your sister!
Brian Good heavens, I'd forgotten all about *her* . . . (*He drifts away below the dining-table*)
Sheila Now! Come along, Carole dear—why don't you open up your suitcase and show me what you've collected so far?

Sheila reaches for the suitcase. Carole keeps a firm hold on it, and they have a small tug-of-war.

Carole No!
Sheila What?
Carole No!
Sheila Don't be silly . . .
Carole No!!
Sheila (*surprised*) What?

Carole Well, you see—the thing is . . .

Fortunately, at that moment Andrew comes back from the hall with Jane.

Jane is about the same age as Sheila, though not as attractive, and has a dry sense of humour. She does not see Brian. Carole is holding her suitcase in her arms like a baby.

Andrew There! You see? I said it would be Jane.

Sheila reacts with alarm, having not yet appraised Jane of the situation regarding Brian, and speaks far too abruptly and far too loudly.

Sheila Jane! You're early! I said twelve-fifteen!

Rather surprised by this welcome, Jane looks at her wrist-watch.

Jane It's nearly half-past.
Sheila It can't be! (*Then she collects herself and crosses to Jane*) Jane darling, how nice to see you! (*As they embrace, she whispers to her urgently*) I must *talk* to you!
Jane (*with a puzzled smile*) That's all right. We'll all be talking during lunch.
Sheila (*apprehensively*) Yes . . .! That's the trouble.

Andrew comes down between them and leads Jane away to Carole, leaving Sheila stranded.

Andrew Now, let me introduce you to Carole!
Jane (*puzzled*) Who's Carole?

Carole looks over the top of her suitcase.

Carole *I* am . . .
Andrew Carole's collecting jumble for the Boy Scouts.
Jane Oh. I'm so sorry. I'm afraid I haven't brought anything with me.
Carole It doesn't matter. Really.

Andrew smiles broadly at a somewhat bemused Jane.

Andrew And now, Jane—we've got a big surprise for you!
Jane For *me*?
Andrew We certainly have. Close your eyes! (*He produces a large coloured handkerchief*)
Jane What?
Andrew Close your eyes! I'll tell you when you can look.

Totally bewildered, Jane allows Andrew to tie the handkerchief over her eyes.

No peeping mind! Now, you come over here and see the lovely surprise we've got for you.

He leads the blindfolded Jane across to Brian.

Well—there he is! (*He indicates Brian with a flourish. Then he looks back to Jane and realizes she is still blindfolded*) It's all right. You can look now.

Jane pulls the handkerchief down from her eyes—and sees Brian. She reacts.

Jane Brian! (*To Sheila*) What the hell is *he* doing here?

They all look at Sheila.

Black-out.

CURTAIN

ACT II

The same. A few minutes later

Sheila is now perched on one of the dining chairs, Jane is sitting on the sofa in a daze, Carole is in the armchair with Brian on the arm of it. Andrew is standing. They all have got drinks

When the curtain rises, they remain silent and motionless, like statues, for a moment. Then they all, in unconscious unison, lift their glasses and sip their drinks

Andrew, obviously disappointed by the lack of enthusiasm for his "surprise" wanders to Sheila. He looks across at Jane, then back to Sheila. He gives a puzzled shrug

Andrew She wasn't very pleased to see him.
Sheila Well, Jane's never very demonstrative. But she *is* pleased. Aren't you, Jane?

Jane awakes from her reverie

Jane What?
Sheila Pleased to see Brian!
Jane (*not too keen*) Well, yes. I suppose so . . .
Sheila Of course you are! You never expected to see him again so soon, did you?
Jane I certainly didn't expect to see him *here*.
Andrew (*puzzled*) Sorry?
Sheila So it was a nice surprise, wasn't it?
Jane It certainly was!
Andrew (*cheering up*) Oh, good. I am glad.
Sheila (*to Andrew*) After all, when they said goodbye to each other on Friday in Florio's, they simply had no idea when they'd see each other again.
Andrew Ah! Yes, of course! (*to Jane*) I suppose *you* thought he was going back to Africa?

A puzzled pause. Jane is totally bewildered, and Brian is sunk in complete confusion.

Jane Africa? I didn't even know he'd been there.

Andrew wanders across to Brian.

Andrew You mean to say you kept it a secret from her, Brian? You clever old chap! So all the time you were in Africa, *she* thought you were in Tunbridge Wells?
Brian (*puzzled*) Why do you keep talking about Africa?
Sheila (*nervously*) Yes, Andrew. You promised not to!

Andrew Ah! Yes! Sorry, Brian. I keep forgetting. You don't want to talk about it in front of other people. Quite understand. I'll try not to mention it again. (*He puts one finger to his lips in a gesture of secrecy*) Sorry. Sorry.

Sheila (*abruptly*) Why don't we all have another drink?

But all glasses are still well charged

Andrew They haven't finished the first one yet. (*He turns to Jane*) So ... how long is it since you saw Brian?

Jane I saw him on Friday.

Andrew No, no. I meant *before* Friday.

Jane Oh. Er—let me see now, it was at a——

Sheila (*intervening quickly*) A long time ago!

Jane What?

Sheila He was very young, wasn't he?

Jane (*a little uncertain*) Was he?

Sheila Oh, yes! Just a child! Running around in shorts!

Jane Shorts? (*She looks across at Brian*) I don't remember seeing you in shorts.

Brian Oh, good. I've got dreadful knees.

He and Carole giggle

Andrew And suddenly there he was walking past your table in the restaurant! It must have been quite a surprise for you.

Jane Yes, it was. I didn't think he'd remember me.

Andrew (*thoughtfully*) Yes, that *was* surprising. I mean, if you hadn't seen him for so long———

Sheila Will you stop asking Jane so many questions! She's not in the witness box. (*Going to Jane, with a nervous laugh*) It's dreadful being married to a solicitor. Every conversation turns into a cross-examination.

Andrew But how on earth did you recognise him in the restaurant when you hadn't seen him since he was a child? (*With a chuckle*) He wasn't *still* wearing shorts, was he?

A moment before Sheila has any inspiration. Then ...

Sheila Well, she'd seen his photographs, of course!

Jane (*surprised*) Had I?

Brian Had she?

Sheila Of course she had! You always sent her photographs.

Jane Did he?

Brian Did I?

Sheila Of course you did! At different stages through the years.

Andrew Short shorts, long shorts and trousers?

Sheila He was always good at sending photographs. Weren't you, Brian?

Brian (*bemused*) I used to be better, but it's got so expensive lately. (*He looks blankly at Carole*)

Carole What are you talking about?

Brian I've no idea! (*He half gets up and looks across at Sheila*) Er—excuse me. I know I'm a bit slow on the uptake and all that, but I wonder if you could———?

Sheila (*to Jane, quickly*) Would you like a cheese football? (*She thrusts a tin of cheese footballs at her*)
Jane I'd rather have another gin . . .
Sheila Yes. of course.

Sheila goes to refill Jane's glass. Brian resumes his seat. Andrew's solicitor's mind is far from satisfied. He sits beside Jane in deep thought, trying to work something out

Andrew Jane . . . Jane . . . H'm . . . these letters you received from Brian. Surely you noticed that they were post-marked Africa and not Tunbridge Wells?

Jane looks at him blankly. Sheila intervenes, hastily

Sheila She never looked at the stamps!
Andrew Didn't she?
Sheila Well, of course not. (*Returning to Jane*) She was far too excited opening the letters. Weren't you, Jane?
Jane Well, I'm always excited handling the mail.

Carole giggles. Jane realizes what she has said, hastily accepts her refilled drink from Sheila, and takes a large sip. Brian raises himself half-way again

Brian Er—excuse me . . .
Andrew H'm?

Brian waves one finger at him, playfully

Brian You're talking about Africa again . . .
Sheila Yes, Andrew. You really must stop. It's a very tender subject.
Brian Is it?
Andrew Yes. Yes, of course. I keep forgetting. So sorry, Brian old chap. I promise not to mention it again. (*He repeats his gesture of secrecy*) Do forgive me.

Brian sits down again

Carole (*to Brian, quietly*) Why does he keep talking about Africa?
Brian I've no idea!

Andrew looks, quizzically, at Jane again. She shifts, uncomfortably, anticipating further cross-examination

Andrew Jane . . . I presume *you* don't have the same reservations about Scotland?
Jane Scotland?
Andrew Yes. I take it *you* don't mind talking about Scotland?

Sheila and Jane, of course, have no idea what he is talking about

Sheila Why on earth should Jane want to talk about Scotland?
Andrew Well, it's not unusual for people to talk about the place where they live.

Sheila and Jane look at each other, blankly. Andrew sees their look and turns to Brian for confirmation

Andrew You did say she lives in Scotland, didn't you?
Brian Who?
Andrew Your sister!
Brian Oh, *her*! Yes. Most of the time.

Sheila realizes, and hastily adjusts

Sheila Oh—I see ! *Brian* told you she lived in Scotland?
Andrew Yes, of course he did. It's not a secret, is it?

Jane sinks her face into her hand

Jane, are you all right?
Jane (*out of her depth*) I was until I came here! (*She drinks some more of her gin*)
Andrew So over lunch Jane can tell us all about her life in the Highlands. (*He smiles at Jane, enthusiastically*)

Jane looks up, apprehensively

Sheila Jane doesn't want to talk about Scotland!
Andrew (*surprised*) I beg your pardon?
Sheila (*restraining herself a little*) She . . . just doesn't want to talk about it.

Andrew rises, getting more and more frustrated.

Andrew Well, if *she's* not going to talk about Scotland, and *he's* not going to talk about Africa, what the hell *are* we going to talk about?
Carole (*looking at him with a smile*) You can always talk about being a solicitor.
Brian Oh, yes! That *is* a good idea!
Andrew (*looking far from pleased at the prospect*) Oh, no, it isn't!
Carole Why not? I'm sure your wife would like to know what goes on in your office.
Andrew No, she wouldn't! She's heard it all before.
Brian Well, *I* haven't heard it all before.
Andrew (*glaring at him*) You wouldn't be interested. It's very dull work.
Brian Not *all* the time, surely?
Carole Don't you have an office party occasionally?
Andrew (*loudly*) No! Never!
Sheila Andrew, there's no need to shout.
Andrew Well, I don't want to talk about work at the weekend. I'd far rather talk about Africa.
Brian Yes, I'm sure you would. But, as a matter of fact——
Sheila Brian! Would you be an angel and go and see to the beef?
Brian What?
Sheila The beef! I'm sure it needs basting.

Brian gets up and goes across to Sheila

Brian Couldn't I just explain about Africa?
Sheila No! Not now! (*Then with a sweet smile she steers him towards the kitchen*) If we use up all our conversation before lunch there'll be nothing left for dessert. Please go and baste the beef.

Andrew He doesn't have to do that. He's supposed to be a guest. I'll do it.

Sheila You may be good at gardening, Andrew, but cooking needs a little more finesse. (*She smiles at Brian*) Thank you, Brian dear. You'll find the oven gloves on top of the fridge. (*Gently but firmly, she propels him out to the kitchen*)

Brian exits to the kitchen

(Turning back to the others with a big smile) Such a nice man

Jane is looking at Sheila and does not notice Andrew approaching her behind the sofa

Andrew Jane!

Jane (*jumping a mile*) I do wish you wouldn't creep up on me like that.

Andrew I can see you're ready for more gin.

Jane Well, there's no need to make me sound like an alcoholic. Yes, I am. (*She hands him her glass*)

Andrew goes to refill Jane's glass

Andrew How about you, Carole?

Carole No, thanks. I'm all right at the moment.

Sheila glances at Andrew's back and then whispers, urgently, to Jane

Sheila I'll explain everything to you in a minute . . .!

Jane Yes, I wish you would!

Andrew You quite sure, Carole?

Carole Yes, but I wouldn't say no to a cheese football.

But nobody obliges

Jane (*aloud*) It was such a surprise seeing Brian here.

Sheila Yes, it certainly was . . .!

Jane (*whispering to Sheila*) I'm *longing* to hear all about Friday.

Sheila What?!

Andrew arrives behind the sofa with Jane's drink

Andrew Jane! Gin!

Jane Oh—thank you. (*She takes it, gratefully*)

Sheila Andrew, are you sure you've finished in the garden?

Andrew (*a little surprised*) Darling, I can't go into the garden now. We've got people to lunch.

Sheila Yes, and I wish we hadn't!

Jane starts to get up

Sheila Oh, not *you*, Jane, of course.

Jane sits again

Andrew Darling, I think *you*'d better have another drink.

Sheila Yes, I think I will. (*She goes quickly to get a drink*)

Deep in thought, Andrew goes slowly to sit beside Jane on the sofa. She watches his approach with apprehension, and takes a big sip of her drink

Andrew Jane . . . Jane . . . er—surely you must have seen your *parents* from time to time?

Jane (*totally lost*) My parents?

Andrew Yes. You must have seen them. Occasionally. Over the years.

Jane Well, I see my mother quite often. She lives in Alfriston. By my father's dead.

Andrew (*outraged*) *Dead*?!

Jane It happens to us all, Andrew.

Andrew Brian really *is* confused. He said they were living in Tunbridge Wells.

Jane *My* parents?

Andrew Yes.

With her drink replenished, Sheila hastily returns to Jane

Sheila Ah—yes! *Your* parents!

Jane What?

Sheila They probably lived in Tunbridge Wells at the time he went to Africa, then your father died and they moved to Alfriston.

Andrew Not much point in moving when you're dead. Even to Alfriston.

Sheila Their mother! *She* moved.

Andrew And forgot to tell Brian about it?

Sheila I expect it slipped her mind.

Andrew (*persisting*) But, Jane . . . your *mother* was still alive. And yet she never told you about Brian going to Africa?

Jane (*totally bewildered*) Why should *my* mother tell me about *Brian* going to Africa?

Andrew (*deeply impressed*) So she kept quiet about what happened? Even from you. Well, I think that's wonderful . . .

Jane I wish I knew what you were talking about.

Carole So do I!

Sheila Yes, Andrew—Carole isn't interested in Africa.

Carole No. I'm more interested in Italy.

Andrew glares at her. She smiles sweetly at him. Sheila goes quickly and enthusiastically to Carole, relieved at the change of conversation

Sheila Oh, good! Let's all talk about Italy. (*To Carole*) Have you ever been there?

Carole Not yet. But I'm going soon. (*She casts a look in the direction of Andrew*)

Sheila Splendid! Which part?

Carole Well, somebody once told me that the Leaning Tower of Pisa looks fantastic in the moonlight.

Sheila Yes, and I'm sure it does. Andrew, you used to go to Italy on business, didn't you?

Andrew (*grumpily*) Yes. But it was different then.

Sheila The Tower must surely still have leaned even when *you* were there.

Andrew abruptly proffers the tin of cheese footballs to Jane

Andrew Would you like a cheese football?
Jane Oh. Thank you, Andrew. (*She takes one*)
Andrew I hope you're not too tired.
Jane It doesn't require much energy to eat a cheese football.
Andrew No, no—I mean, you don't fancy a lie down or something?
Jane What?
Andrew Quick nap before lunch? Freshen you up a little.
Jane Do I look as bad as all that?
Andrew No, no! I mean all that travelling. Must by very tiring for you.
Jane (*bewildered*) Well, my car's quite comfortable, Andrew. And it is only about thirty miles.
Andrew Thirty miles? From Inverness?
Jane No. From Hemel Hempstead.
Carole Could *I* have a cheese football?

Without taking his eyes off Jane, Andrew holds out the tin of cheese footballs. Sheila, also keeping her eyes on Jane, takes it from him and passes it to Carole. Carole settles down in the armchair with them

Andrew Brian seemed to think you were travelling from Scotland.
Jane Why should I be travelling from Scotland when I live in Hemel Hempstead?
Andrew Hemel Hempstead? I thought you were living in——
Sheila (*abruptly*) You forgot the marrow!

They all look at her in surprise

Andrew What?
Sheila The marrow! You forgot the marrow. For lunch.
Andrew I thought we were having peas.
Sheila We are. But we need a marrow as well. (*She pulls him to his feet*)
Andrew Why?
Sheila To make the joint go further. All these extra people arriving for lunch.
Andrew Well, I'm not sure that I've got one that's quite——
Sheila I thought you were so proud of your marrows? You're always bragging about them.
Andrew Yes, I know, but——
Sheila All right! Let's see one, then!
Andrew (*reluctantly*) Oh, very well . . . (*Heavy-footed, he crosses towards the patio*)
Sheila Carole can give you a hand.
Andrew I *can* manage a marrow!
Sheila If they're as big as you say, I would have thought it would take two of your to carry one.
Andrew Oh, all right, then.

Sheila smiles, encouragingly at Carole

Sheila Carole, dear . . .

Carole goes across to Andrew, intent on her cheese footballs. They head towards the garden, Andrew grumbling

Andrew I dunno . . . this is supposed to be Sunday. Day of rest. Bit of gardening, a couple of gins, roast beef and fall asleep in front of the telly . . .

Sheila You must try not to get into a rut, Andrew.

Andrew I *like* being in a rut!

Sheila (*firmly*) The marrow, darling!

Andrew stumbles out into the garden. Carole follows him

Sheila goes to Jane, urgently

Sheila Jane, I'm *so* sorry! You must be terribly confused, but I didn't get the chance to explain. You see, the thing is——

Jane is gazing at Sheila with a broad smile

Jane Well! What about *you*?

Sheila Sorry?

Jane I didn't think you'd invite Brian out here. Not when Andrew's at home!

Sheila I didn't invite him! He just . . . turned up. (*She looks, anxiously, towards the kitchen*)

Jane How exciting!

Sheila It's not exciting at all. All I wanted was a quiet Sunday at home . . .

Jane Oh, no, darling. This is much more fun! Come on, then—what happened?

Sheila When?

Jane On Friday, of course!

Sheila (*nervously*) What do you mean?

Jane Well, *I* only know what happened in the restaurant. What about afterwards?

Sheila Afterwards? There wasn't any "afterwards"!

Jane You don't expect me to believe that, do you?

Sheila It's true! (*She casts another anxious look towards the kitchen*) Oh, Jane . . . why did you let me go off in a taxi with Brian?

Jane Well, he *was* going in your direction.

Sheila Was he?

Jane (*with a smile*) And *you* seemed to be going in *his* . . .!

Sheila (*ignoring the innuendo*) There's nothing wrong in travelling in a taxi with somebody.

Jane No—no, of course not. Provided you sit well apart and keep upright.

Sheila (*appalled*) Jane!

Jane Oh, come on—you know how I love a bit of gossip. What happened?

Sheila Nothing!

Jane Then you've nothing to worry about.

Sheila Well, don't say it like that!

Jane Like what?

Sheila As if I *did* have something to worry about.

Jane Well, you did rather encourage him in the restaurant.

Sheila That doesn't mean I encouraged him in the taxi!

Jane So he just . . . took you to the station?

A pause

Sheila What?
Jane (*suspiciously*) He *did* take you to the station, didn't he?
Sheila Y-yes . . . Yes, of course!
Jane (*smiling, knowingly*) Ah! But not straight away . . .?

Sheila hesitates. Another look towards the kitchen. Then she shakes her head, miserably

Sheila No . . .
Jane (*smiling, delightedly*) Ah-ha! twice round the park?
Sheila No!
Jane Then where did he take you?
Sheila He . . . he took me back to his flat.

Jane stares, frozen in surprise, for a moment or two

Jane His *flat*?
Sheila (*shiftily*) Yes . . .
Jane I thought he lived in Amersham.
Sheila He's got a flat in London, as well.
Jane How exciting! Well, go on—don't keep me in suspense! What happened?
Sheila I told you—nothing!
Jane *Nothing*?
Sheila Yes.
Jane Nothing nothing or something nothing?
Sheila Nothing nothing!
Jane So why did you go back to his flat?
Sheila For coffee.
Jane And did you get it?
Sheila What?
Jane Coffee.
Sheila Yes, of course!
Jane And how long did you stay there?
Sheila Oh . . . about an hour and a half.
Jane Sorry?
Sheila More or less.
Jane You must have drunk a hell of a lot of coffee in that time!
Sheila No. I . . . I fell asleep.
Jane (*smiling hopefully*) Exhausted?
Sheila Too much wine!
Jane And when you woke up?
Sheila He called me a taxi and I went to the station and caught my last train.
Jane (*disappointed*) And . . . nothing nothing?
Sheila No. (*A pause, then . . .*) At least, I don't think so.
Jane You mean you don't remember?!
Sheila I told you—I'd had too much to drink.
Jane I couldn't bear to think that something might have happened to *me* and I didn't remember. No wonder you invited him over today!

Sheila Jane . . .!

Jane Well, you did say that Andrew was going away on business this weekend, didn't you?

Sheila Er . . . yes. Yes, he—he *was* . . .

Jane There you are, then! It was going to be the ideal time. Oh, what a pity he changed his mind and everything went wrong . . .

Sheila Nothing went wrong! (*Trying hard to remember*) And I'm sure I didn't invite him here . . . (*She has a sudden thought*) Anyway— *you* were coming to lunch!

Jane Yes, but you could have rung me up and put me off—and then used me as an alibi.

Sheila (*appalled*) Jane! What a thing to suggest!

Jane That's what friends are for, darling.

Andrew and Carole's voices are heard out in the garden. Jane reacts in alarm

Good heavens! Here they are and you haven't put me in the picture yet! I'm not at all sure who I'm supposed to be . . .

Andrew and Carole come back in from the garden with a large vegetable marrow

Andrew (*proudly*) There you are! What about that?

Sheila Oh, yes, that *is* a big one, isn't it? (*She takes the marrow from him*) Come on, Jane! Let's go into the kitchen.

Andrew We'll *all* end up in the kitchen at this rate.

Sheila I've got to cope with lunch, haven't I?

Andrew It doesn't take three to baste the beef. Not unless we're roasting the whole animal.

Sheila And what about the marrow? We can't eat it like this, you know.

Sheila and Jane make for the kitchen. Sheila hangs back at the door

We shan't be long. I'm sure you two can find lots of things to talk about. Carole can tell *you* all about jumble sales, and you can tell *her* all about Italy. (*She goes off into the kitchen*)

Carole sits on the sofa, finishing off the cheese footballs

Andrew I wish you'd stop going on about Italy . . .

Carole (*eating*) *You* went on about it enough at the office party.

Andrew (*awkwardly*) Well . . . there were extenuating circumstances.

Carole You mean you'd had too much to drink and you fancied me?

Andrew No!

Carole What?

Andrew Well . . . yes, I suppose so . . .

Carole (*warmly*) You said such nice things to me . . .

Andrew D-did I?

Carole That's why I'm here. (*She gazes at him, adoringly*)

Andrew (*flustered*) Well, you—you obviously misunderstood and—and imagined that I—that I *meant* what I said.

Carole I thought solicitors always did.

Andrew (*after a nervous glance towards the kitchen*) Look, Carole—if I stepped out of line at the office party, I—I do apologize.

Carole Don't apologize! I liked it!

Andrew Well, you shouldn't have done! And you shouldn't have come here today. So please get the next train back to London. You really can't stay here for lunch!

Carole But I'm hungry!

Brian comes in from the garden, a big saucy smile on his face

Brian And what were you two doing at the bottom of the garden?

Andrew I thought you were in the kitchen!

Brian I was. But then I spotted you from the window and went out to see what you were up to.

Andrew We weren't up to anything!

Carole He was just showing me his marrow. (*She giggles*)

Sheila comes in from the kitchen and sees Brian

Sheila Oh, there you are, Brian! Every time I think you're in the kitchen you've disappeared into the garden.

Brian I went to watch the march of the marrow. (*He grins at Andrew*)

Sheila Well, don't stay in here. I need some help out there.

Carole I'll come.

Sheila No, Carole, dear. You stay here and talk to Andrew. Come along, Brian!

Andrew But he's basted the beef. Surely that's enough to be going on with?

Sheila (*somewhat put out*) Oh. Well, later on I shall need some help with the Yorkshire pudding.

She gives an anxious look and goes back into the kitchen

Andrew I don't know what's got into Sheila today. She doesn't usually cook by committee.

Carole Are there any more cheese footballs? I've nearly finished these.

Brian You won't need any lunch after that lot.

Andrew No, you won't! So you may as well go home *now*! (*He tries to pull her to her feet*)

Brian Don't be silly! She didn't come all the way to Little Buckden just for cheese footballs.

Andrew Didn't she?

Brian (*enjoying himself*) It's all right, Andrew. I know *all* about it.

Andrew I—I don't know what you're talking about!

Brian Oh, come on! *You* know where she's going, don't you?

Andrew Of course I don't know where she's going!

Carole Well, you can guess, can't you?

Brian Yes. You must have played guessing games at office parties.

Carole And not only guessing games, either! (*She giggles*)

Andrew I've no idea where she's going!

Brian (*impressively*) She's going . . . to Italy!

Andrew Don't be ridiculous. She's hardly likely to take a suitcase full of jumble all the way to Italy.

Brian Ah! But it's not *really* full of jumble, is it?

Andrew Isn't it?

Brian No, of course it isn't. You know that, and I know that. Don't we?

Andrew Do we?

Brian Of course we do! It's full of clothes, isn't it?

Andrew Clothes?! In a suitcase?

Brian All neatly packed. Ready for the off!

Andrew The off?

Brian To sunny Italy! (*He sings a snatch of a Neapolitan air*) And what's more—she's not going alone.

Andrew (*flustered*) Well, I didn't expect she would be. Not many people do.

Brian My Aunt Amy did. She went alone to Clacton every year. Then she met a sailor on shore leave from the Portuguese Navy and went off with him.

Carole Where is she now?

Brian Living in Sesimbra, I think. (*To Andrew*) Who do you think she's going with?

Andrew You told us. A Portuguese sailor.

Brian Not my Aunt Amy—Carole!

Andrew I don't see that it's any of our business! Carole is perfectly free to go away with anyone she likes, and I think it's very rude to pry into her affairs like this.

Sheila looks in from the kitchen, wearing oven gloves

Sheila Andrew, I hope you're not asking Brian a lot of questions.

Brian (*reassuringly*) No, it's all right. We're talking about Italy.

Sheila Oh, good! (*She comes in a little*) I really do need some help to mix the batter for the Yorkshire pudding.

Carole Oh, *I* can do that. (*She goes to Sheila*)

Sheila No, no! I'm sure Brian's much better at batter.

Carole But I must do *some*thing to help! Why should Brian do everything? After all, I am a girl.

Brian Yes. There's no doubt about that. Is there, Andrew?

Sheila (*reluctantly*) Oh—well—all right. Come along, then, Carole.

Sheila and Carole go out into the kitchen, Sheila casting an anxious look back as she goes

Brian She's such a nice girl, isn't she? So pretty and delightful.

Andrew Yes . . .

Brian Lucky fellow!

Andrew What?

Brian beams with delight. Andrew is keen to change the subject, uncertain whether Brian knows anything

You ready for another drink?

Brian Oh. Thanks.

Andrew (*abruptly*) Help yourself, then! (*He sits on the sofa*)
Brian Right. (*He goes to get himself a drink*)

Andrew is thoughtful, his solicitor's mind re-asserting itself. After a moment . . .

Andrew I . . . I thought you told me she was coming from Scotland.
Brian Who?
Andrew Your sister.
Brian Oh. Yes. She is.
Andrew No, she isn't.
Brian What?
Andrew Hemel Hempstead.
Brian No. Inverness.
Andrew Hemel Hempstead.
Brian Look—I should know where my own sister's coming from!
Andrew You should, but you obviously don't. You can take my word for it.
Brian (*coming down with his drink*) Hemel Hempstead?
Andrew Yes.

A pause

Brian How do you know all this?
Andrew Well, she told me, of course.

A pause

Brian My sister told you?
Andrew Yes.
Brian Really? I didn't know she'd been on the telephone . . .

A pause

Andrew Did she never mention it in one of her letters?
Brian Mention what?
Andrew Hemel Hempstead.
Brian No. And it's not the sort of place you'd forget to mention, is it? (*He chuckles*)
Andrew Wouldn't have thought so. I suppose she thought it wasn't important. But in her photographs, didn't you notice that the background was Surrey and not Scotland

Brian looks blank. He sits beside Andrew

Brian What photographs?
Andrew Well, *you* sent photographs to *her*. Surely she returned the compliment and sent some out to you in Africa?
Brian I've never *been* to Africa!

Andrew looks at him for a long time in silence

Andrew Don't be ridiculous.
Brian It's true! That's why I couldn't understand you going on about it all the time.

Andrew But Sheila said you'd been there for years.

Brian I can't imagine what gave her that idea.

Andrew considers the ramifications for a moment in silence. Then . . .

Andrew Does that mean, then, that you've never been in any 'trouble', either?

Brian What sort of trouble?

Andrew Well . . . financial.

Brian Good Lord, no! I've still got a little in the bank.

Andrew (*puzzled*) But you and I were going to talk about it after lunch. Man to man. I offered to give you some advice. Surely you remember that?

Brian Yes. But I didn't know what you were talking about! Why should you think that I was in financial trouble?

Andrew Because Sheila told me!

Brian Oh. Did she? Ah . . .

Andrew Sheila seems awfully confused about a lot of things today.

Brian Yes—yes, she does, doesn't she?

Andrew I wonder why . . .?

Anxious to change the subject, Brian leaps to his feet, nervously, and looks at his watch

Brian Good heavens! She's taking her time!

Andrew (*looking a little surprised*) Who?

Brian My sister! If she's only coming from Hemel Hempstead she should have been here by now.

Andrew Are you feeling all right?

Brian When you spoke to her, did she say what time she'd be arriving?

Andrew Arriving? She's already here!

Brian Already where?

Andrew Out there in the kitchen, of course!

Brian Really? (*He goes and has a quick look into the kitchen*) No, she isn't. There's just the three of them out there—Sheila, Carole and Jane.

Andrew Exactly. Sheila, Carole and your sister Jane.

Brian Jane's not my sister!

Andrew She isn't?

Brian Good Lord, no! I only met her at a press party three weeks ago. It was Jane who introduced me to Sheila on Friday.

Andrew Then why on earth should Sheila tell me that Jane was your sister?

Brian Sheila told you that?

Andrew Yes.

Brian Oh. Oh, I see . . .!

Sheila and Carole come in from the kitchen. Carole is carrying the now empty cheese football tin

Sheila Jane insists on making an apple crumble. Isn't that splendid? (*She sees their set faces*) I hope you two have had a nice chat about Italy.

Andrew (*grimly*) Italy, Scotland, Africa, Tunbridge Wells and Hemel Hempstead.

Sheila Oh, that must have been very interesting.

Andrew Fascinating! Considering some of us have never been to *any* of those places!

Sheila Well, that's what conversation is all about, Andrew. Finding out about other people and other places.

Andrew (*loudly*) We've certainly been doing that! How about Africa, for a start?

Sheila (*serenely*) If this is an example of how you behave in Court, I'm very surprised you win *any* of your cases. Please forgive my husband's behaviour, Carole. When you get to Italy at least the men there will now how to treat a lady.

Carole Oh, yes. I've heard about that. All pasta and pinching.

Sheila No, dear. That isn't quite what I meant. Good heavens, you've finished all the cheese footballs! (*She takes the empty tin from her*)

Andrew Brian's never even *been* to Africa!

Sheila (*attempting to carry it off*) Don't be silly, Andrew. I saw a photograph of him in shorts standing in front of Mount Kilimanjaro. A picture that could hardly have been taken in the middle of Richmond Park.

Andrew (*heavily*) And what about his *sister*?

Sheila (*quickly going to Brian*) Brian, perhaps you'd take Carole out into the garden and show her the artichokes?

Brian Yes—rather!

Carole I don't like artichokes!

Brian You don't have to like them—just look at them!

Brian hustles her out into the garden

Sheila is left with the empty tin. Andrew looks at her, bewildered

Andrew Why on earth did you tell me that Jane was Brian's sister?

Sheila Because she *is*!

Andrew Not according to Brian.

Sheila avoids his eyes. He goes to her, peering closely

Sheila . . .?

Sheila H'm?

Andrew How much wine did you drink the other night?

Sheila (*without thinking*) Quite a lot. (*She corrects herself quickly*) Not very much.

Andrew Quite a lot.

Sheila (*holding up the empty tin*) She's eaten all the cheese footballs.

Andrew Sheila—I'm waiting. Why did you make up all those stories about Brian? You must have had a reason.

Sheila puts the empty tin down on the table and regroups her forces

Sheila Er . . . because I . . . I didn't want you to know the truth. I didn't think it would be fair.

Andrew Fair to who?

Sheila It'll be very embarrassing.

Andrew No more embarrassing than talking about Africa to somebody who's never been there.

Sheila (*turning to look at him*) Well, if I tell you, will you promise not to say anything?

Andrew Won't that seem rather rude? Sitting through Sunday lunch in silence.

Sheila (*in one breath*) I mean will you promise not to say anything about what I'm going to tell you if you insist on my telling you and I do?

Andrew All right. Go on, then.

He waits for the big revelation. Sheila crosses away below him, gathering herself. She takes a deep breath and says . . .

Sheila Jane . . . is *not* Brian's sister.

A pause. Naturally, he remains impassive at this not very surprising statement

Andrew Yes. I know that. Go on.

Sheila prepares yet again

Sheila Brian . . . is *not* Jane's brother.

Andrew Yes. That follows logically from your previous statement.

Sheila They're not related at all!

Andrew (*patiently*) H'm . . .

Sheila turns and explodes her bombshell

Sheila They're having an affair.

Andrew is astonished

Andrew (*loudly*) An affair!

Sheila Sh'sh!

Andrew (*incredulously*) Brian and Jane?

Sheila Yes.

Andrew (*starting to laugh*) Don't be ridiculous! (*He laughs*) Brian and——? (*And laughs*) Oh, dear, oh, dear . . . (*And laughs*) Why didn't you tell me before?

Sheila You can see why I didn't tell you before! You'd have been laughing all through lunch.

He tries to control himself, and looks at her in disbelief

Andrew Brian and Jane?

Sheila Yes.

Andrew Good Lord! Well, I never. That explains it, then.

Sheila (*relieved*) Does it? Oh good.

Andrew Well, well, well! Good old Jane! (*He chuckles happily*)

Jane comes in from the kitchen, carrying a glass of sherry

Andrew laughs even louder when he sees her. Jane looks slightly taken aback

(*Playfully*) Ah! I see you're helping yourself to the sherry now! (*He laughs*)

Jane What's the matter with you?

Andrew (*trying to control himself*) Oh, nothing—nothing at all! Everything all right in the kitchen?

Jane (*puzzled by his behaviour*) Yes, I think so. I've put the apple crumble in.

Andrew Oh, good! (*He turns to Sheila, unable to control his mirth*) Did you hear that, darling? Everything's all right out there. Gas burning. Water boiling. Fat jumping. Apple crumbling. Everything as it should be. Roast beef. Yorkshire pud. Everything splendid.

Jane Are you feeling all right, Andrew?

Andrew Never better!

Jane hastily finishes off her sherry to help her to act it up a bit

Jane Now—where has my brother got to?

Sheila looks pained. Andrew only laughs even more

Andrew Your—your brother?!

Jane He was here a moment ago. He hasn't gone back to Africa, has he?

Andrew Africa! Oh, dear me! (*He collapses on to the sofa, unable to control his laughter*)

Sheila (*trying to intervene*) Jane, dear . . .

But Jane is now well into her stride

Jane I simply couldn't believe it when he walked into that restaurant on Friday. It was such a lovely surprise!

Andrew Yes, it would be! (*He laughs and laughs*)

Sheila Jane, dear . . .

Jane continues remorselessly, having been primed by Sheila in the kitchen

Jane I shall have to ring up Mummy and Daddy after lunch and tell them he's here.

Crying with laughter, Andrew reaches for the telephone receiver

Andrew I should do it now if I were you! It's not far from Tunbridge Wells. If they drive very fast they'll be here in time for your apple crumble!

Sheila struggles with Andrew for the telephone receiver, succeeds in getting it back from him and goes above the sofa to replace it

Jane It'll be so nice for the whole family to be together again.

Andrew Isn't that going to be rather difficult? You said your father was dead!

Jane (*undeterred*) We're still a family. Daddy may be gone, but he's still with us in spirit.

Sheila (*trying desperately to stem the torrent*) Jane!

Jane (*to Andrew*) He hasn't changed a bit, you know.

Andrew He must have done by now! (*He wipes the tears from his eyes, but cannot stop laughing*)

Jane Not my father! Brian! He looks just the same now as he did when he went abroad.

Sheila *Jane!* Andrew doesn't want to hear about that!

Jane (*puzzled*) I thought you told me he did.

Sheila Not any more.

Poor Jane cannot understand why she is being stopped when she is doing so well

Sheila Andrew, aren't you going to open the wine?
Andrew What?
Sheila The wine!
Andrew Ah—yes. Right. (*He gets up and heads for the hall*) I'll see to it. I'll open it. Give it a chance to breathe. Shan't be long. (*Chuckling happily, he turns before he goes and looks at Jane*) You know, you do look different!

He goes out into the hall, laughing

Jane Whatever's the matter with him?
Sheila I expect he's hungry.
Jane (*a little hurt*) Why did you stop me? I though I was doing rather well.
Sheila Yes, but the situation's changed since then.
Jane You mean I'm not Brian's sister any more?
Sheila No.
Jane Ah. Does *he* know that?
Sheila Who?
Jane Andrew.
Sheila Yes. Brian told him. (*She sits on the sofa avoiding Jane's eyes*) So I . . . I just had no alternative. I had to tell him the truth.
Jane (*going to her, surprised*) You told him about Brian fancying you in the restaurant on Friday?
Sheila (*evasively*) Well, I . . . I didn't put it quite like that. I mean, I wouldn't want to upset Andrew.
Jane No, of course not. (*A pause*) How *did* you put it?
Sheila Well, I . . . I sort of—wrapped it up a little.
Jane He's taking it very well. Doesn't seem at all upset. Quite the contrary in fact. Did you tell him *everything*?
Sheila Well, I don't *know* everything, do I?
Jane (*remembering*) Ah—no, of course not. So there's only one person who *does*.
Sheila Who?
Jane Well—Brian, of course! Presumably *he*'ll remember what happened! You'll have to ask *him*.

Sheila looks alarmed at the prospect

Brian and Carole come back in from the garden

Brian We've looked at the artichokes.
Carole They seem to be getting bigger every minute.
Jane (*going briskly to Carole*) Well, now I'll show you the bathroom.
Carole Why should I want to see the bathroom?
Jane Because lunch will be ready soon and you'll need to wash your hands. (*She takes Carole by the hand and sweeps her off towards the hall*) Come along, Carole!

Jane gives Sheila a knowing look and goes off with Carole into the hall. As they go, they meet Andrew coming back with the wine. He sees Jane and immediately starts laughing again. He goes off to the kitchen with the wine, laughing happily, Jane and Carole react and go

Sheila and Brian are alone. She sits in silence, unsure of how to approach the truth she seeks. Brian moves to her

Brian I'm awfully sorry.
Sheila (*alarmed*) What about?
Brian About being Jane's brother. I should have realized.
Sheila Oh, that . . .
Brian I was a bit slow on the uptake.
Sheila And I didn't get the chance to tip you off. You kept disappearing.
Brian Oh, well. No harm done, eh?
Sheila That remains to be seen . . . (*She shifts, nervously*) Brian . . .
Brian Yes?
Sheila There's something worrying me . . .
Brian Oh, there's nothing to worry about.
Sheila Isn't there?
Brian No. There's masses of food for five.
Sheila Not about the food!
Brian Oh.
Sheila About you . . . and me.
Brian Ah . . .
Sheila Will you put my mind at rest?
Brian What about?
Sheila About last Friday! In your flat.
Brian Ah . . .
Sheila What *did* happen?
Brian Do you really want to know?
Sheila Yes!

He appears to be about to impart some momentous information and prepares himself accordingly

Brian Well . . . (*pause*) . . . I gave you a cup of black coffee . . .
Sheila Yes? And then . . .? Did we——?
Brian Kiss each other? Oh, yes!
Sheila We did?!
Brian Well, *I* kissed *you*, and you didn't seem to mind.
Sheila (*avoiding his eyes again*) And . . . and then . . .?
Brian And then . . . (*he gives another elaborate look around*) . . . and then I gave you another cup of black coffee.

Sheila looks a little hurt

Sheila Why? Didn't you want to go *on* kissing me?
Brian Oh, yes. I wanted to go on all right! But—well—you'd had rather a lot to drink, so I couldn't be sure that you knew what you were doing, and you might have regretted it.
Sheila (*her eyes lighting up*) So we didn't . . .?
Brian (*shaking his head, regretfully*) No. I'm afraid not. You fell asleep.
Sheila (*looking rather ashamed*) Fell asleep?! How very rude of me. How long for?
Brian Three-quarters of an hour. Then you woke up and insisted on going

home. So I called you a taxi, you said thank you and kissed me good-night and went off to the station to catch your train.

Sheila And that was *all* that happened?

Brian (*smiling enigmatically*) What do *you* think?

Sheila Oh—Brian!

Relieved, she kisses him briefly on the mouth as . . .

Jane and Carole come in from the hall and see them. Jane's face lights up as she jumps to the wrong conclusion

Jane Ah! you got your answer, then, Sheila? You lucky old thing!

Andrew comes sailing in from the kitchen. He is carrying a tray on which are five glasses and a bottle of champagne. He is beaming with joy

Sheila looks at him in horror

Andrew Well—here we are, then!

Sheila (*going to him, urgently*) Andrew! Have you gone mad? What's that?

Andrew Champagne!

Sheila I know what it is but why is it here?

Andrew I just brought it in! (*Laughing happily, he sets the tray down on the dining-table and proceeds to open the bottle*)

Sheila This is Sunday lunch, not a wedding reception. Take it away at once.

Andrew Don't be silly. We're having a celebration. Aren't we, Brian? (*He winks at Brian, knowingly*)

Brian (*puzzled*) Are we?

Andrew You bet we are! After all, this is a special occasion. Isn't it, Jane?

Jane (*puzzled also*) Is it?

Andrew (*grinning at her saucily*) You know—I'd never have guessed.

Jane Guessed what?

Andrew Some people certainly are dark horses. (*He opens the bottle*) There we are! (*He starts to pour the champagne*)

Carole (*to Jane*) What's he talking about?

Jane I've no idea. But I never say no to champagne.

Sheila (*apprehensively*) Andrew, I hope this hasn't got anything to do with what I talked to you about.

Andrew Of course it has! Brian, would you pass these around, there's a good chap?

Brian Oh—right. (*He takes two glasses to Carole and Jane*)

Carole I wish I knew what everyone's talking about . . . (*She sits on the sofa*)

Sheila (*to Andrew, urgently*) What I told you was entirely confidential.

Andrew Yes, I know. (*Laughing*) But I never could keep a secret!

Brian returns to Sheila and Andrew

Brian (*to Sheila*) What have you been telling him?

Sheila Never you mind! (*to Andrew*) You promised not to say anything.

Brian (*to Andrew*) What has she been telling you about?

Andrew About *you*, of course! (*He laughs, helplessly*)

Brian (*nervously*) About me?

Andrew Yes! Sheila told me all about it.

Brian (*looking at Sheila in surprise*) You *told* him?

Sheila (*helplessly*) Well . . .

Brian (*to Andrew*) And—is that what we're celebrating?

Andrew Certainly!

Brian (*astonished*) You mean you don't *mind*?

Andrew Of course I don't mind. I'm rather surprised, but I don't mind. Why should I?

Brian Well, I thought you might be a *bit* upset.

Andrew Good heavens, no! It's the sauciest thing I've heard for a long time!

Brian is at a loss to understand Andrew apparent joyful condoning of his wife's relationship with him. He turns to Sheila

Brian So you needn't have worried after all.

Jane (*her champagne poised*) Are we allowed to drink or do we have to wait for the starting gun?

Andrew Well, I would just like to say a few words——

Sheila (*quickly*) No, you wouldn't!

Andrew Wouldn't I?

Sheila What I told you I told you in confidence, and I shall be very upset if you say anything about it at all.

Andrew cannot understand her objections

Andrew But *four* of us know about it already.

Carole Well, it must be *you* four, 'cos I know nothing!

Sheila I positively forbid it!

Andrew (*disappointed*) Well, it's going to be a bit of an anti-climax if I don't propose a toast . . .

Sheila All right, then—you can propose a toast——

Andrew (*cheering up*) Oh, good!

Sheila —but don't say what you're proposing it *to*!

Andrew (*grumpily*) Oh. All right. Won't be much fun, though. (*He raises his glass*) Here's to . . . you know what.

They all raise their glasses

All To . . . you know what. (*They all drink, solemnly*)

Carole I wish *I* knew what . . .

Brian (*grinning at Andrew*) Of course, it's really a double celebration, isn't it, old boy?

Andrew (*warily*) Is it?

Brian Yes! You know—Carole going off to Italy any minute.

Andrew's bonhomie suffers a mortal blow

Sheila Don't be silly, Brian. Carole can't be going to Italy *today*. She's busy collecting jumble.

Brian Sheila—she isn't *really* collecting jumble.

Sheila Isn't she?

Brian No.

Sheila Then what the hell has she got in her suitcase?

Jane (*to Carole*) What the hell have you got in your suitcase?

Brian (*knowingly*) *I* think she's got pretty little dresses, brief bikinis, naughty nighties . . .

Sheila (*outraged*) And nothing for the Boy Scouts?

Brian Certainly not!

Sheila (*to Carole, confused*) But if you weren't collecting jumble for the Boy Scouts, why on earth did you come all the way to Little Buckden with your suitcase?

Brian (*with heavy innuendo*) Well, she's not going *alone*, is she?

Sheila What are you talking about?

Brian She's going with a man who *lives* in Little Buckden!

Andrew reacts and puts the bottle down noisily on the tray. They all look at him in surprise

Sheila (*to Carole*) A man who lives in Little Buckden?

Carole Yes!

Sheila Then why on earth are you having lunch with *us* and not with *him*?

Carole (*puzzled*) Sorry?

Sheila I've got a wonderful idea! Ring him up and ask him to join us for lunch. (*She lifts the receiver*)

Andrew There isn't enough!

Sheila Of course there's enough. Your marrow's enormous. Come along, Carole. What's his number?

Andrew She doesn't know!

Sheila She's going to Italy with a man and doesn't know his telephone number?

Andrew He's not *on* the telephone!

Sheila (*replacing the receiver*) Then you'd better get the car out, Andrew, and go and fetch him.

Andrew He hasn't finished packing yet!

Sheila You seem to know a lot about Carole's boy-friend.

Brian (*quietly*) You bet he does . . .! (*He grins at Carole*)

Sheila If we fetch him now he can join us for champagne.

Andrew There isn't any left!

Sheila Yes, there is. There's still some in the bottle.

Andrew I'm saving that for Christmas!

Sheila You must forgive him, Carole. We can only assume that he's saving his manners for Christmas as well.

Andrew There's no more room at the table! We'll be cramped enough as it is.

Brian Oh, I dunno. If Carole's boy-friend does come, I doubt if we'll notice the difference.

Andrew glares at him

Sheila Come along, Carole. I'll drive the car myself.

Andrew No!

Sheila What?

Andrew He's—he's very shy! Isn't he, Carole? (*He gives her a frantic look*)

Carole (*hiding a smile*) Yes, he certainly is! Perhaps I'd better meet him *after* lunch . . .

Andrew Good idea!

Sheila Oh. Very well. But it does seem a shame. We'd like to have met him. Wouldn't we Andrew?

Andrew Come on! Don't hang about! Finish off the champagne!

Sheila Andrew—champagne is meant to be sipped.

Andrew Well, sip it, then—but sip it quickly!

Jane *I* already have. (*She goes to Andrew*) Is there a tiny drop more?

Andrew There is for *you* ! (*He refills her glass, grinning at her*) After all, this sort of thing doesn't happen every day, does it?

Jane What a pity. I love champagne. (*She starts to go*)

Andrew Don't go away.

Jane (*hesitating*) I beg your pardon?

Andrew (*smiling secretively*) You *are* allowed to stand next to him, you know.

Jane Who?

Andrew Brian, of course!

Jane (*mystified*) I'm quite happy over here, thank you very much. (*She returns to sit beside Carole, and they giggle together*) What *is* he talking about?

Carole I've no idea.

Brian goes and puts one arm around Andrew's shoulders in a heavily man-to-man relationship

Brian Well, I must say, Andrew—I'm very pleased that *you're* so pleased. It does make it a lot easier for us.

Andrew I don't see that it makes any difference. What you two get up to in private is entirely your own affair. Eh, Jane?

Jane Sorry? I don't quite——

Sheila (*sensing danger*) Jane! Come on!

Andrew (*to Brian*) They're off to the kitchen again!

Jane (*rising*) Where are we going?

Sheila To the kitchen, of course!

Andrew (*to Brian*) What did I tell you?

Andrew and Brian laugh

Sheila Come along, Jane!

Andrew Take the rest of the bottle with you, Jane.

Jane Oh, thank you, Andrew. (*She takes the bottle of champagne from him*)

Andrew After all— *you*'ve got something to celebrate!

Jane goes off to the kitchen, grateful for the champagne but puzzled by Andrew's remarks

Sheila hangs back at the kitchen door, anxiously

Sheila Oh, Brian—don't pay any attention to anything Andrew may say when I'm out of the room. He's not quite himself today.

She smiles, nervously, and goes out to the kitchen

Carole gets up, having seen something

Carole Oh, there are some more over here! (*She climbs up the bookcase*)
Andrew What?
Carole (*delightedly*) Cheese footballs!
Andrew Oh, good.

He exchanges an amused look with Brian. Carole gets a new tin of cheese footballs from the bookshelf and settles herself down in the armchair. Brian takes Andrew to the sofa, and they both sit down

Brian Well, I must say, Andrew old chap—it's a great relief.
Andrew Is it?
Brian I was quite nervous, I can tell you. I mean, I couldn't be sure how you'd react when you heard about us, could I? (*He laughs and pats Andrew cosily on the knee*)
Andrew Well, it isn't something I feel very strongly about.
Brian (*puzzled*) No—I know—and I can't understand it . . .
Andrew Doesn't make any difference, as far as I can see. I mean, it's of no great importance to *me*, is it?
Brian (*appalled*) No great importance to you? Even though she came back to my flat the other night?
Andrew (*smiling blandly*) Did she do that? Good Lord. I *am* surprised. (*He chuckles happily*) Well, well, well . . .
Brian (*gazing at him in disbelief*) And it still makes no difference to you?
Andrew (*casually*) No. Of course not.
Brian (*morally outraged*) Good God, man! She was there for an hour and a half!
Andrew Better and better! She really is a dark horse, isn't she?

Brian simply cannot believe Andrew's incredible tolerance

Brian And you still don't mind?
Andrew Of course I don't mind.
Brian (*patting Andrew on the knee*) We British really are wonderful, aren't we?

A pause. Andrew looks at him

Andrew What's that got to do with it?
Brian Well, if this had happened anywhere else in the world—your Latin countries, for instance—the situation would have been inflammatory.
Andrew (*looking at him blankly*) Don't see why. You're perfectly free to have an affair with whoever you like. Provided you don't do it in the street and frighten the horses.

Carole emerges out of the tin of cheese footballs

Carole Oo, I say! Is that what you've been doing, Brian? Frightening the horses?
Brian (*giving her a hard look*) Just get on with your cheese footballs, eh?
Carole I only asked . . . (*She goes back to her cheese footballs*)
Andrew So, as far as I'm concerned, Brian—you carry on! (*He pats Brian on the knee just as Brian did to him a moment ago*)

Brian (*surprised but grateful*) Oh. Jolly good. Right. (*He pats Andrew on the knee*)

Carole Here—do you two want to be left alone?

Brian gives her a look. She wilts

I'll just get on with my cheese footballs . . . (*She carries on eating*)

Brian Of course, at that time I didn't know about *you*.

Andrew What about me?

Brian Well, I mean—(*he grins, playfully*)—you've got plans of your own, haven't you?

Andrew Have I?

Brian Yes. You know!

Carole (*without looking up*) Oh, he knows all right. He just didn't think that *you* knew.

Andrew Knew what?

Brian About you going off to Italy with Carole.

Andrew (*going quickly to Carole*) You didn't tell him that, did you? (*He grabs the tin of cheese footballs from her rather abruptly, causing a lot of them to fall onto the floor. He goes on to his hands and knees and crawls about picking them up*)

Carole I didn't need to tell him. He guessed.

Brian I just put two and two together.

Andrew Well, you got the wrong answer! I am *not* going to Italy with Carole!

Brian relaxes on the sofa, confidently complacent

Brian Well, you may as well. Not much point in your staying here, is there?

Andrew Of course there is. I've got things to see to in the garden.

Brian There's no point in your mooning around the garden being miserable. You may as well pop off with Carole, now that you know about *us*. It's only fair.

Having collected up the fallen footballs, Andrew gets to his feet

Andrew Why on earth should I pop off to Italy with my secretary simply because a total stranger has been having an affair with a friend of my wife's? (*He hands the tin of cheese footballs back to Carole*)

Brian loses confidence and remains silent for a moment, thinking hard

Brian I beg your pardon?

Andrew Well, for the life of me I can't understand why you should expect me to change my plans and go off to Italy with Carole—however attractive that idea may be—simply to make you feel less guilty about what you may or may not have done with Jane.

A dreadful pause

Brian With *Jane*?

Andrew begins to sense that he has misunderstood the situation

Andrew Isn't that what you were talking about?

Brian (*uncomfortable*) Er—well, no. Not exactly.
Andrew *Not* you and Jane?
Brian No. Not me and *Jane*.

A pause

Andrew (*suspiciously*) Somebody else?

Brian says nothing. Andrew realizes the truth

Good Lord . . .! You don't mean——
Brian (*miserably*) I thought you *knew* . . .

Andrew gazes at him, incredulously

Andrew My *wife*?
Brian (*quietly*) Yes . . .
Andrew Good Lord . . . (*Quite a pause as the truth sinks in*) But you only
    met her on Friday.
Brian Yes . . .

A pause

Andrew No wonder she fell over her slippers.
Carole (*nervously*) I think I'd better go and help in the kitchen . . .
Andrew There's no need for that. There's not going to be a scene, if that's
    what you're worried about. As Brian said, we are British. We do know
    how to behave in a crisis. (*He goes to get himself a large whisky*)
Carole (*to Brian*) I just knew you were up to something. I could tell.

Andrew returns with his drink and looks at Brian, incredulously

Andrew And you really thought I wouldn't mind? About *that*?
Brian (*miserably*) Well . . . you see . . . I thought you were going off to Italy
    with Carole.
Andrew And that balanced everything up?
Brian Well . . . yes, I suppose so.
Andrew I'm surprised you didn't advertise in *Exchange and Mart*. (*He prowls
    away with his drink like a caged lion*) So why on earth did you come here
    today? You were bound to bump into me.
Brian (*rising*) I didn't know *you* were going to *be* here!
Andrew Must have been a nasty surprise for you then when you discovered
    I was out there in the garden with my boots on.
Brian Yes, it was!
Andrew No wonder you were so keen to make the coffee.
Brian I simply thought that Sheila and I were going to have lunch together.
Andrew And that was *all* you were going to have together? Just lunch?
Brian Well . . . yes.
Andrew You surely don't expect me to believe that on the strength of a casual
    meeting in a restaurant you spent a summer Sunday travelling all the way
    out here simply to have lunch? After all, you did say you took her back
    to your flat, didn't you?
Brian (*ruefully*) Ah—yes—I did, didn't I? That was silly of me. (*He tries*

to cover quickly) It was on the way to the station! We just popped in for a quick cup of coffee.

Andrew An hour and a half, you *said*!

Brian (*defensively*) Yes, but she slept most of the time!

Andrew Slept?!

Brian Yes. She was . . . tired. So she slept.

Andrew And what happened *before* she slept?

Brian Nothing! We just talked. You know how people talk. We just talked. We had a nice conversation. She's a very interesting woman.

Andrew Oh, good.

Brian And very attractive. A nice, interesting, attractive woman.

Andrew Yes, I know!

Brian And I fancy her.

Andrew I should jolly well hope so. So do I! (*He throws back his whisky and goes for a refill*)

Carole (*to Brian, quietly*) You're daft, you are. You should have met her for lunch somewhere else.

Brian Yes, I wish I had!

Andrew And that was the only reason you came to lunch. To talk?

A beat

Brian Well . . . no. There was *another* reason . . .

Andrew turns with his drink, his hackles rising again

Andrew I thought so!

Brian No! Not what *you* think! I came to bring these.

He produces a pair of ear-rings from his pocket. Andrew comes down to look at them, heavily suspicious

(*helpfully*) They're ear-rings.

Andrew (*testily*) I know what they are! (*He peers at them more closely*) These belong to Sheila. I gave them to her. Christmas before last.

Brian Well, she took them off and left them behind.

Andrew (*balefully*) In your bedroom, I suppose?

Brian No! In the restaurant! She left them on the table in the restaurant.

Andrew (*doubtfully*) Oh, yes?

Brian Yes! I noticed them as I was leaving and picked them up to give them to her on the way out.

Andrew But you *didn't* give them to her.

Brian No. I . . . I forgot.

Andrew Yes. I bet you did! Had "other things" on your mind, I suppose? Couldn't wait to get her back to your place, could you? How do I know she took these off in the restaurant? She *could* have taken them off in your flat!

Brian Yes. She could. But she didn't.

Andrew I've only your word for that, haven't it?

Brian (*enigmatically*) Yes—I suppose you have . . .

A brief pause as they look at each other. Then . . .

Andrew I'll ask her! (*He starts for the kitchen*)
Carole Oh, I don't think you should do that.

Andrew stops, turns and looks at her, somewhat surprised by her intervention

Andrew I beg your pardon?

Carole gets up and joins Brian

Carole (*coolly*) Well, if I were you, I wouldn't say anything about it at all.
Andrew Why not?
Carole Well—*she* doesn't need to know that *you* know anything about it, does she? Wouldn't that be kinder? After all, she is your wife.

Andrew holds her look for a moment, undecided. Then . . .

Andrew Oh, No! I shall ask her all right! (*He sets off again, purposefully*)
Carole Well, in that case——

Andrew stops again

—*we*'ll have to tell Sheila all about you and me going to Italy. Won't we, Brian?

Brian links arms with Carole and they both smile delightedly

Brian Yes! We certainly will!
Andrew (*staring at them, helplessly*) But I wasn't *going* to Italy.
Carole (*smiling triumphantly*) She doesn't know that, though, does she?
Andrew (*gazing at them in disbelief*) You wouldn't do that?
Brian We certainly would!
Carole Yes! We certainly would!

   Sheila comes in from the kitchen

Andrew slips the ear-rings into his pocket

Sheila Lunch won't be very long.

Andrew looks at her, seething, longing to confront her; but manages to control himself

   Andrew, I hope you've been entertaining everybody.
Carole Yes, he certainly has!

Andrew takes a pace towards Sheila, simmering, about to erupt

Andrew Now, look here, Sheila—there's something I——

Brian starts to sing 'O Sole Mio' and mimes the action of a gondolier. Andrew stops and looks back at Brian and Carole, uncertainly

Sheila Oh, Andrew, would you be an angel and get some mint for the potatoes? Brian couldn't find it, but I'm sure *you* know where it is.
Andrew Of course I know where it is!
Carole Well, go and get it then!
Andrew There's something I want to know first——!
Brian Don't say you've forgotten where you planted it?

Andrew Of course I haven't forgotten!
Carole I'll come and help you find it.
Andrew I haven't lost it!

He stomps out into the garden

Carole smiles at Brian, and follows Andrew out

Brian wanders, thoughtfully, towards Sheila

Brian Now, I wonder how Andrew found out that Jane and I were having an affair . . .

She smiles, a little shamefaced

Sheila Well . . . I had to tell him *some*thing, didn't I?
Brian Yes. I suppose you did.
Sheila And, you know, the extraordinary thing is—he actually believes it!

Brian manages to look her straight in the eye

Brian Yes—he does, doesn't he?

Jane comes briskly in from the kitchen, looking towards the garden

Jane Carole isn't leaving, is she?
Sheila No, of course not. She's just helping Andrew look for the mint.
Jane Oh, that's all right, then. I thought perhaps she was going off and forgetting her tickets.
Sheila What tickets?
Jane Her air tickets. To Italy. I saw them lying about in here somewhere. (*She looks around*)
Sheila (*surprised*) In here? Why on earth should they be in here? Surely Carole's gentleman-friend will have them with *him*.

Brian, anxious for Sheila to be kept in ignorance about Andrew and Carole, looks apprehensively

Brian Yes, of course he will!
Jane Well, I could have sworn I saw them in here . . .
Brian Don't be ridiculous! They couldn't possibly be in here!
Jane Perhaps they're under the newspapers . . . (*She starts to look amongst the Sunday newspapers on the sofa*)
Brian (*going to her quickly*) No! They aren't! There are no air tickets there! None at all! Give those to me! (*He grabs the newspapers from Jane abruptly*)

Sheila and Jane look astonished by his behaviour

Sheila Brian, whatever's the matter with you?
Brian Nothing's the matter with me! It's *her*! She's looking for tickets and there aren't any. (*He tries to laugh it off*)
Jane I know I saw them somewhere . . . (*She notices the magazines on the armchair table*) Ah! Perhaps they're over there.

Jane heads for the magazines. Brian rushes across and beats her to them, snatches up the magazines and clutches them to his bosom, protectively, and sits on the edge of the armchair

Brian They aren't here, either! No tickets! Nothing! Nothing at all. Just magazines. Nothing but magazines.

Jane wanders above the sofa, still looking

Sheila Brian, there's no need to get so excited.
Brian Oh, yes, there is . . .!

Jane spots the tickets on the sofa table, peeping out from under a magazine

Jane Aaaaah! *There* they are!
Brian What?! (*In his alarm, he slips and sits heavily on the floor in front of the armchair, dropping the magazines as he does so*)
Jane (*holding up the tickets, triumphantly*) I knew I'd seen them in here somewhere.

Sheila moves to Jane, smiling mischievously. Brian gazes at them, helplessly, from his position on the floor

Sheila Jane—I wonder who she's going with . . .
Jane (*playfully*) Shall we look and see?
Brian No—you musn't!
Sheila But if he lives in Little Buckden it might be somebody we know. Come on, Jane . . .
Brian No!!
Sheila (*surprised at his vehemence*) What?
Brian I don't think you should do that!
Sheila Don't be silly, Brian. You're making such a fuss. We won't tell anyone. But it would be rather fun to find out who Carole's going with. Wouldn't it, Jane?
Jane It certainly would.

Sheila and Jane giggle in anticipation, as Sheila starts to open the first ticket

Brian I don't think you should read other people's tickets!

Sheila sees the name on the first ticket, smiling happily

Sheila Well, that one's *hers* . . . (*She starts to open the second ticket*)
Brian (*scrambling to his knees*) Jane! Don't just stand there! Stop her!
Jane Why? *I* want to know, too.
Sheila *Now*, then . . . (*She opens the second ticket and sees Andrew's name on it. The laughing stops. A dreadful pause. Then she looks up from the ticket. Icily*) Well—what a *lovely* surprise . . .! So *that's* why she came here with her suitcase.

She hands the ticket to Jane. Jane looks at it, and reacts

Jane Oh, my God . . .! (*She hastily hands the ticket back to Sheila, and starts to go towards the kitchen*)
Sheila Where are you going?
Jane I think I smell burning . . .!
Sheila No, Jane! You stay here. (*With relish*) You don't want to miss *this*.
Jane Oh, yes, I do! I never could stand the sight of blood.

And she scuttles off to the safety of the kitchen

Sheila turns to look at Brian. He gets to his feet, sheepishly

Sheila So *that*'s what all the fuss was about. You knew all the time, didn't you?

Brian (*shrugging helplessly*) Yes, but I didn't want *you* to know.

Sheila That was very sweet of you, Brian. (*Then, with relish*) But you needn't worry about me. I'm going to enjoy this . . . !

Carole comes in from the garden with some mint

Sheila looks at her with a smile that could slice bacon. Carole senses that all is not well

Sheila Aah! *There* you are, Carole!

Carole holds out the mint, meekly

Carole We found it . . .

Sheila What?

Carole (*nervously*) Mint. For the new potatoes.

Sheila Have you left Andrew hiding in the garden?

Carole He's . . . he's just coming.

Sheila (*with relish*) Oh, good!

Carole moves towards Brian, and sees from his expression that the cat is well and truly out of the bag

Well! We *are* going to have a lot to talk about over lunch, aren't we?

Carole I don't think I'm very hungry . . .

Sheila I'm not surprised. You're full of cheese footballs!

Brian Sheila . . . I wouldn't say anything to Andrew about this, if I were you.

Sheila (*rounding on him, eyes blazing*) Well, you are *not* me! *I* am! And I intend to speak to him the moment he comes in from the garden, and I doubt if I shall stop for at least five minutes!

Brian (*firmly*) Well, *I* don't think you should say anything about it at all.

Sheila Why not? I'm looking forward to it.

Brian and Carole exchange a look

Carole Well . . . in that case . . . *we*'ll have to tell Andrew what happened between you and Brian. Won't we, Brian?

Brian links arms with Carole. They both smile, delightedly

Brian Yes! We certainly will!

Sheila stares at them helplessly

Sheila But nothing happened between us!

Brian How do you know? You said you didn't remember.

Sheila You *told* me!

Brian I might have made it up.

Sheila (*trying to reassure herself*) Nothing happened! You know it didn't! (*Then uncertainly*) Did it?

Brian (*with a shrug*) Maybe it did. Maybe it didn't. But even if it didn't, *he* doesn't know that, does he?

Sheila (*gazing at them in disbelief*) You wouldn't do that?

Brian (*smiling broadly*) We certainly would!

Carole Yes! We certainly would!

Sheila—like Andrew before her—can only stare at their triumphantly smiling faces

Andrew comes in from the garden

Sheila hides the tickets behind her back and looks at him, smouldering, like Vesuvius about to erupt

Sheila You found it all right, then?

Andrew is puzzled by her tone, but decides to ignore it

Andrew Oh, yes. I knew exactly where it was, you see.

Sheila And, anyhow—Carole was there to help you, wasn't she?

Andrew (*sensing the frost in the air*) H'm?

Sheila We were just talking about Carole's *boy*-friend.

Andrew (*warily*) Really?

Sheila Fancy dragging her all the way to Little Buckden on the public transport. And with a heavy suitcase, too! I can't think why he didn't arrange to meet her at the airport like a proper lover. (*With mounting anger*) I can only assume that he's a very inconsiderate man—a man who thinks only of himself!

Andrew Oh, I wouldn't say that . . .

Sheila (*getting into her stride*) Well, I would! I can just imagine the kind of man he is——

Brian intervenes firmly

Brian I don't think you should, though, Sheila.

Sheila stops, in full flood, and looks at him

Sheila I beg your pardon?

Brian Well, I don't think you should say anything at all about Carole's boy-friend.

Carole No, neither do I! After all . . . one thing could lead to another. Couldn't it, Brian?

Brian It certainly could!

Brian and Carole smile, delightedly. Sheila decides to remain silent

Come along, Carole! Let's see to the potatoes. (*He starts for the kitchen, hesitating near to Sheila*) Is it all right if I do the carving? I haven't had roast beef for ages. (*He continues towards the kitchen*)

Carole (*a sudden thought*) Brian . . .

Brian Yes?

Carole Have *you* ever been to Italy?

Brian No, as a matter of fact, I—— (*He realizes what she is suggesting*) Oh, good heavens . . .!

He grins and goes, quickly

Carole Brian . . .! Brian!

She pursues him out to the kitchen

Sheila and Andrew are left in a vacuum. Neither can quite look at the other

Andrew Nice, entertaining young people . . .
Sheila Yes. I do hope they don't *talk* too much during lunch.
Andrew So do I . . .!

A pause. They are both undecided whether to divulge what they each now know about the other, but their fear of reprisals is too strong. Andrew goes to pick up the fallen magazines from the floor in front of the armchair

Well . . . mustn't let the roast beef spoil, eh?
Sheila No. That would never do.

Sheila brings the air tickets out from behind her back and looks at them, thoughtfully, for a moment. She cannot resist the temptation, and moves down to where Andrew is collecting up the magazines. She bends down, picks up a magazine and hands it to him. He takes it without looking and puts it on the armchair with the others. The same with a second magazine. Then Sheila passes him the air tickets. Automatically, he starts to put them with the other magazines. Then he sees what they are and stares at them, blankly. Sheila waits for his reaction, enjoying the situation

Andrew (*innocently*) What are these?
Sheila Air tickets.
Andrew H'm?
Sheila (*more precisely*) Air tickets.
Andrew Oh.
Sheila I think they belong to you.
Andrew *Do* they?
Sheila Well, one of them's got your name on it.
Andrew Has it, really? Good Lord . . . (*After a pause*) Am I going somewhere?
Sheila (*icily*) Not any more! (*She grabs the tickets back from him*)
Andrew Look—I can explain.
Sheila Yes, I *bet* you can! (*She starts to go*)
Andrew (*casually*) Sheila . . .

She stops, half-way to the kitchen

Sheila Well?
Andrew I tell you what, I'll explain *those* . . . if you'll explain *these*. (*He produces the ear-rings from his pocket and holds them out to her, without looking in her direction*)

Sheila sees them and comes back to him to get a closer look. She smiles, innocently, pleased to see them

Sheila Oh, good! My ear-rings! I thought I'd lost them. Where were they?
Andrew They were where you left them. (*He looks at her and delivers the coup de grâce*) In Brian's bedroom.

Now Sheila does not know what to believe!

Sheila What?!

A brief pause. Then slowly, and rather sheepishly, she hands the air tickets back to him. Andrew hands the ear-rings to her in return. The music starts to play—"Sunday, sweet Sunday, with nothing to do . . ." They smile at each other, happy and relieved. He leans forward and they kiss, lightly, and then start to move towards the kitchen, his arm around her. As they go, Andrew throws the air tickets, with abandon, over his shoulder. The music swells as they go, happily, towards the kitchen, and——

—The CURTAIN *falls*

FURNITURE AND PROPERTY LIST

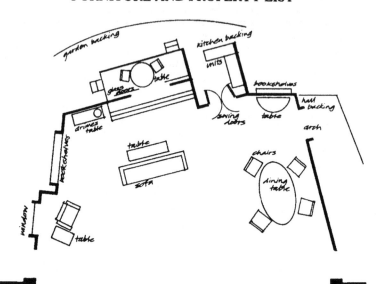

ACT I

On stage: Sofa. *On it:* Sunday newspapers

Sofa table. *On it:* telephone, transistor radio, ashtray, magazines, 3 napkins, tin of cheese footballs

Armchair. *Behind it:* **Andrew's** shoes

Coffee table. *On it:* magazines

Dining-table

4 dining chairs

Drinks table. *On it:* bottles of whisky, gin, sherry, tonics, various glasses, lamp (non-practical)

Crescent table. *On it:* lamp (non-practical)

Bookshelves. *On them:* books, ornaments, tin of cheese footballs

Patio doors open

On patio:

Garden table

2 garden chairs

Sun umbrella (unopened)

Potted plants

Off stage: 3 wine glasses, glass-cloth (**Sheila**)
Bunch of flowers (**Brian**)
3 knives, 3 forks, 3 dessert spoons, 3 dessert forks (**Sheila**)
Pepper and salt (**Sheila**)
Tray with 3 coffee cups and saucers, pot of coffee, sugar-bowl,
  cream-jug, plate of biscuits (**Brian**)
Suitcase, handbag containing 2 air tickets (**Carole**)

Personal: **Sheila:** wrist-watch
Brian: wrist-watch
Andrew: wrist-watch, large coloured handkerchief
Jane: wrist-watch

ACT II

Strike: Suitcase
Handkerchief

Set: 5 glasses with drinks

Check: Air tickets under magazines on sofa table

Off stage: Large marrow (**Andrew** and **Carole**)
Tin of cheese footballs (**Carole**)
Oven gloves (**Sheila**)
Empty cheese footballs tin (**Carole**)
Glass of sherry (**Jane**)
2 bottles of red wine (**Andrew**)
Tray with bottle of champagne, 5 champagne glasses (**Andrew**)
Sprig of mint (**Carole**)

Personal: *As Act I plus:*
Brian: ear-rings in pocket

LIGHTING PLOT

Practical fittings required: nil
Property fittings required: 2 table lamps
A drawing-room and garden patio. The same scene throughout

ACT I, A summer morning

To open: Bright sunshine

Cue 1   **Jane:** ''What the hell is *he* doing here?'' They all look at Sheila   (Page 35)
        Black-out

ACT II, A summer day

To open: Bright sunshine

No cues

EFFECTS PLOT

ACT I

Cue 1   **As CURTAIN rises**   (Page 1)
Music on transistor radio—vocal version of "Sunday, Sweet Sunday" from "Flower Drum Song"

Cue 2   **Brian** switches off transistor radio   (Page 1)
Cut music

Cue 3   **Brian:** "... living in Tunbridge Wells"   (Page 15)
Doorbell rings

Cue 4   **Sheila:** "*I* didn't hear anything"   (Page 15)
Doorbell rings

Cue 5   **Andrew:** "... the sound of it by now"   (Page 15)
Doorbell rings

Cue 6   **Sheila:** "... things for the Boy Scouts"   (Page 32)
Doorbell rings

Cue 7   **Andrew** gives **Brian** a funny look, puzzled by his manner   (Page 33)
Doorbell rings

ACT II

Cue 8   **Andrew** hands the ear-rings to **Sheila**   (Page 69)
Fade in music—vocal version of "Sunday, Sweet Sunday" from "Flower Drum Song"

Lightning Source UK Ltd.
Milton Keynes UK
UKOW05f0111100217

294074UK00001B/65/P